THE CITY:

ITS SINS AND SORROWS.

RECENTLY PUBLISHED.

THE GOSPEL IN EZEKIEL.

BY THE REV. DR. GUTHRIE.

12mo. $1 00.

"Usually happy in their selection of foreign works for republication, the Messrs. Carter have never done a wiser thing for themselves, nor a better thing for the community, than in reproducing for American readers the fine eloquence of the greatest living preacher in Scotland. No such stirring sermons have issued from the press in this country since the time of President Davies. At times you may be ready to charge the preacher with extravagance; at times you may quarrel with his theology as hard, illogical, and, on some points, self-contradictory; but, after all, you will confess that never was your heart more thoroughly moved by the truths of the gospel than through the vivid images, the impassioned appeals, the burning words of these twenty sermons, combining as they do the peculiarities of Ezekiel and of Paul. Would that New York had ten such preachers as this light of the Free Church in Edinburgh. We have read the book with tears."—*Independent.*

"If our clergy desire to see how the most intense evangelicalism can be presented with all the freshness of a spring morning; if they desire a book which they may study as a model from which to preach to persons who live in the nineteenth century, then let them buy this work. If our laity desire a book of sermons, not dull or uninteresting, they will find it here. We predict for this book a large sale."—*South. Churchman.*

"Dr. Guthrie is one of the most able and eloquent scholars of the Free Church in Scotland. The twenty sermons of which this volume is composed, at once settle the fact that he is the greatest preacher in that land of keen, intrepid theologians. We by no means endorse every doctrinal position, or approve every turn of the rhetoric. And yet we can most heartily commend the volume for its downright Christian earnestness, its depth of moral conviction, its strong, fresh thought, its impassioned brilliance, and terse, pungent style."—*Gazette.*

THE CITY:

ITS SINS AND SORROWS.

BEING A SERIES OF SERMONS FROM LUKE XIX. 41.

"He beheld the city, and wept over it."

BY

THOMAS GUTHRIE, D.D.
AUTHOR OF THE "GOSPEL IN EZEKIEL," ETC.

NEW YORK:
ROBERT CARTER & BROTHERS,
No. 530 BROADWAY.

1857.

STEREOTYPED BY
THOMAS B. SMITH,
82 & 84 Beekman-street.

S. B. THOMSON,
BINDER,
82 & 84 Beekman-st.

PRINTED BY
E. O. JENKINS,
26 Frankfort-st.

THE CITY:

ITS SINS AND SORROWS.

SERMON I.

"He beheld the city, and wept over it."—LUKE xix. 41.

ONE evening as Saul returned to Gibeah with his cattle from their distant pastures, the lowing of his herd was lost in a wail that grew loud and louder as he drew near the city. Some mischief has happened. Amazed and alarmed, he hurries forward to find the people all dissolved in tears—distracted by some public grief. What can have happened? Bathed in golden sunset, Gibeah from her mountain seat looked quietly down on the green vale of Jordan, away to the shores of the Dead Sea. He saw no occasion whatever tor this terrible turmoil. He saw nor dead nor dying. Why, then, do the men pluck their beards, the women with dishevelled hair and long loud wail beat their naked breasts, and the very children, moved by sympathy and infected with the general grief, mingle their own with their parents' tears? Since morning, when he left the city, a messenger, who sped on flying feet, had arrived, breathless, from Jabesh-Gilead. He brought alarming tidings. He tells Saul's townsmen that unless they and the country will rise to the rescue, the city must open her gates to the Ammonites, and submit to the most barbarous cruelties. Ignorant of this, nor seeing occasion for their sorrow, Saul, on whom the Spirit of the Lord was about to descend, that he might rise an avenger and deliverer of the oppressed, demanded to know the cause of this frantic grief. He said:—"What aileth the people that they weep?"

The same question may be asked regarding the Saviour's tears on the occasion to which my text refers. A mighty crowd was rolling down upon Jerusalem from the sides of Olivet.

On they came, rending the air with acclamations. With prophetic ear, and five centuries before, Zechariah had heard these shouts, and catching them, where he stood upon the heights of prophecy, he shouted back again to the jubilant multitude:—"Rejoice greatly, O daughter of Zion, shout, O daughter of Jerusalem, behold thy King cometh unto thee. He is just, and having salvation, lowly and riding upon an ass." Now I can fancy one of that crowd—who was near enough our Lord to see the tears upon his cheek—with greater surprise than Saul, asking John or Peter, or some other one of the twelve, who formed all the body-guard of this King, What aileth Jesus that he weeps? In such an hour, what makes him sad? Did ever king thus enter his capital—on the eve of his coronation thus present himself to a joyous people? What ails him? What would he have? The nation renders him every honor. His enemies being witnesses, the whole world is gone after him. The palm trees yield their branches, the men their robes, the women their admiration, the whole multitude their voices, as they pour their hearts into the joyous cry:—"Hosanna, Hosanna, blessed be he that cometh in the name of the Lord." Why, then, that shadow on his thoughtful brow, that deep expression of sorrow on his face—in his eyes these starting tears? Everything smiles on Jesus. The day is auspicious. Jerusalem has come out to welcome her long expected King. The whole scene is bathed in sunshine, nor is there a cloud in all the sky of his smiling fortunes to account for this shower of tears. What aileth Jesus that he weeps? There must be some secret grief, that, overflowing the deep fountains of his heart, runs out at his eyes in these streaming tears. There was.

Often coveted yet fatal power! he foresaw the future. But however eventful to this world were the next three days, it was not on their sad scenes and circumstances that his weeping eye was fixed. Down in that garden, by the glare of midnight torches, that flashed and flickered amid its hoary olives, he saw a prisoner bound fast with cords; in yonder judgment hall, that towered conspicuous above the other buildings, he saw a captive, arrayed in the mockery of purple, and bearing on his brow a thorny crown; in that long street which wound through the city, he saw one exhausted by brutal usage, and pale with loss of blood, fainting, falling beneath a cross; and on a distant mount, which rose beyond Jerusalem, by the light of what seemed a dying sun, he dimly saw a mangled form hanging on the fatal tree. In these figures, which presented themselves in affecting and terrible succession, the "seer" saw himself—none around to weep for him but some kind women, nor any to confess him but a dying thief. Is it for this he weeps? No. He looked over the intermediate events, onward to the future of forty years.

The curtain rose. Jerusalem was before him. "He beheld the city;" not as now with the tide of business, but the roar of battle in its streets—torn by contending factions, and Cæsar thundering at the gates—brother, staggering from the famine-struck house, to strike his sword into a brother's bowels—the holiest laws of nature horribly reversed: not infants living on the fountain of a mother's breast, but mothers—famished, miserable, maddened mothers, feeding upon their own offspring; the breached and battered walls manned by living skeletons; the streets resounding with the groans of the dying, and choked with the festering bodies of the dead. How miserable the aspect of Jerusalem! He beholds scenes of sufferings, which, as described by an eye-witness, are without a parallel even in the annals of the most savage wars. Nor does the curtain fall on the stage of this tragedy of many terrible acts, until the Roman torch has wrapped the city—body and limbs, the house of David, and the house of God—in one red winding sheet of flame, and the Roman plough has buried her guilty ashes in the silent earth.

It was these, the guilt of Jerusalem and the sufferings of his countrymen, that were in Jesus' eye. Hence this sorrow and these tears. Hence, on another occasion, that most touching burst of pity, patriotism, and piety : "O Jerusalem, Jerusalem, how often would I have gathered thy children together as a hen gathereth her chickens under her wings, and ye would not. Behold, your house is left unto you desolate." And at a time, when we should have expected, that through the selfishness inherent to suffering, his own sorrows would have absorbed all his feeling, hence also that tender but ominous advice to the women who bewailed and lamented him:— "Daughters of Jerusalem, weep not for me, but for yourselves and children." Restrain your grief, keep your tears for a future occasion, reserve them for yourselves, for the babe unborn, the child that hangs upon your breast.

When Pontius Pilate—that unhappy time-server—brought out our Lord before the infuriate multitude, perhaps he cherished the hope, that the pitiful sight would calm their passions, as Jesus' voice did the blustering winds and rude waves of Galilee. And we are told, that as Jesus appeared, "wearing the crown of thorns and the purple robe," Pilate appealed to them, saying:—" Behold the man." These words of a scene, which even in its rudest painting, we cannot study without emotion—although like oil poured, not on the stormy waters, but the roaring fire, they only increased and intensified the cry of "crucify him, crucify him,"—may be applied with propriety to the scene before us. "He wept." This was not a God weeping—God cannot weep. These were not angels' tears—for angels never weep. In them, in the sad expression on his blessed face, I say with Pilate:—"Behold the man!" the veritable man, bone of our bone, flesh of our flesh, soul of our soul, heart of our heart, strung by the same hand and tuned to the same harmony as our own. How precious are these sorrows! They attest his perfect manhood. They assure us of his sympathy, when we attempt to lay bare before you the evils of our city, and rouse you to arrest and amend them. They warrant us to expect a blessing from him who loved his kindred as a man, and his country as a patriot. From heaven he watches our fight with the powers of darkness, and regards with applauding eye all—the humblest as well as highest laborer—who, sighing and crying "for the abominations that are done in the land," labor to leave the world, their native country, or the city of their habitation, somewhat better than they found them.

Before we unveil the evils that call for tears, and, as we shall by and by show, call for some thing else than tears, let us—

1*st. Look at the city in some of its favorable aspects.*

This earth's earliest city was built by a murderer. Its foundations, I may say, were laid in blood. Enoch was its name, Cain was its founder. Those who, living far from the din and bustle of cities, read with a wonder that grows into horror, the dark record of their courts and crimes; those, who see in the blasting effect of their murky air on flower, and shrub, and tree, only an emblem of their withering influence on the fairest human virtues; those simple cottagers, who, tremblingly alive to their danger, saw a son or a daughter leave home for the distant city, and have received her back from a Magdalene, or him from a prison, to expire in the arms of forgiving, but broken-hearted affection, they may fancy that the curse of the first murderer and their first founder hangs over earth's cities — dark, heavy, as their cloud of smoke.

We can excuse them for thinking so. Great cities some have found to be great curses. It had been well for many an honest country lad, and many an unsuspecting young woman, that hopes of higher wages and opportunities of fortune, that the gay attire, and polished tongue, and gilded story of some old acquaintance, had never turned their steps cityward, nor lured them away from the rude simplicity but safety of their rustic home. Many a foot that once lightly pressed the heather or brushed the dewy grass, has wearily trodden in darkness and guilt and sin these city pavements. Happy had it been for many that they had never exchanged the starry skies for the lamps of the town, nor had ever left their lonely glens, or quiet hamlets, or solitary shores, for the throng and roar of our streets—well for them, that they had heard no roar but the river's, whose winter flood it had been safer to breast; no roar but ocean's, whose stormiest waves it had been safer to ride than encounter the flood of city temptation, which has wrecked their virtue and swept them into ruin.

Yet I bless God for cities. . I recognise a wise and gracious providence in their existence. The world had not been what it is without them. The disciples were commanded to "begin at Jerusalem," and Paul threw himself into the cities of the ancient world, as offering the most commanding positions of influence. Cities have been as lamps of light, along the pathway of humanity and religion. Within them science has given birth to her noblest discoveries. Behind their walls freedom has fought her noblest battles. They have stood on the surface of the earth like great breakwaters, rolling back or turning aside the swelling tide of oppression. Cities indeed have been the cradles of human liberty. They have been the radiating, active centres of almost all church and state reformation. Having therefore no sympathy with those who, regarding them as the excrescences of a tree or the tumors of disease, would raze our cities to the ground, I bless God for cities. And before addressing you on their evils, will advert to some of their advantages.

First, *The highest humanity is developed in cities.*

Somehow or other, amid their crowding and confinement, the human mind finds its fullest, freest expansion. Unlike the dwarfed and dusty plants which stand around our suburban villas, languishing, like exiles, for the purer air and freer sunshine that kiss their fellows far away in flowery field and green woodland, on sunny banks and breezy hills, man reaches his highest condition amid the social influences of the crowded city. His intellect receives its brightest polish where gold and silver lose theirs—tarnished by the searching smoke and foul vapors of city air. The finest flowers of genius have grown in an atmosphere where those of nature are prone to droop, and difficult to bring to maturity. The mental powers acquire their full robustness where the cheek loses its ruddy hue, and the limbs their elastic step, and pale thought sits on manly brows, and the watchman, as he walks his rounds, sees the student's lamp burning far into the silent night. And as aerolites—those shooting stars which, like a good man on his path in life, leave a train of glory behind them on the dusky sky—are supposed to catch fire by the rapidity of their motion, as they rush through the higher regions of our atmosphere, so the mind of man fires, burns, shines, acquires its most dazzling brilliancy, by the very rapidity of action into which it is thrown amid the bustle and excitements of city life.

Second, *The highest piety is developed in cities.*

It is well known that the most active tradesmen, the most vigorous laborers, the most intelligent artisans, the most enterprising merchants, are to be found in cities. And if, just as in those countries where tropical suns and the same skies ripen the sweetest fruits and deadliest poisons, you find in the city the most daring and active wickedness, you find there also—boldly confronting it—the most active, diligent, zealous, warm-hearted, self-denying, and devoted Christians. No blame to the country for that. Christians are like soldiers—it is easier fighting in the regiment, where the men stand shoulder to shoulder, than standing alone to maintain some solitary outpost. Christians, to use a familiar figure, are like coals, or firebrands—they burn brightest when gathered into heaps. Christians are like trees—they grow the tallest where they stand together; running no small chance, like a solitary tree, of becoming dwarfed, stunted, gnarled, and bark-bound, if they grow alone. You never yet saw a tall and tapering mast which, catching the winds of heaven in its outspread wings, impelled the gallant ship on through the sea, and over the rolling billows, but its home had been the forest—there, with its foot planted upon the Norwegian rock, it grew amid neighbors that drew up each other to the skies. So is it with piety. The Christian power that has moved a sluggish world on, the Christian benevolence and energy that have changed the face of society, the Christian zeal that has gone forth, burning to win nations and kingdoms for Jesus, have, in most instances, been born and nursed in cities. To the active life and constant intercourse which belong to them, religion has owed her highest polish, and that freedom from peculiarities and corners, which the stones of the sea-beach acquire by being rolled against each other in the swell and surf of daily tides.

In rural districts, with all their natural and ever-fresh charms, a good man often finds a weary loneliness; and where fields, and hills, and long miles separate him from church and Christian neighbors, it needs an extraordinary measure of the grace of God to make his life of comparative isolation "a solitude sweetened." Give me the city with Christian neighbors at my door, and daily intercourse with genial and congenial spirits. If I fall, I have them there that will help me up; if I flag, I have them there that will help me on; if two are better than one, twenty are better than two; and with such opportunities of Christian fellowship as the city only affords, my circumstances there are much more allied to those of the saints in glory, than his whose lot is cast amid the distant and scattered homes of rural scenes. He often has to pursue his journey through the desert—so far as human intercourse is concerned—all but alone, a solitary pilgrim to Canaan. Manifold as are their evils, their temptations, and their snares, it is only in cities that piety enjoys the full benefit of the truth, "as iron sharpeneth iron, so doth the face of a man his friend."

Third, *The highest happiness of saints is found in city life.*

Man is a social as well as domestic being. His arms may not, but his heart can embrace more than a family. His nature is social. His religion is social. And as the earth's loftiest peaks rise not in their snows on some isolated hill that stands like a lonely pyramid on the level plain, but where the mountains, as in the Alps, or Andes, or Himalayan range, are grouped and massed together, so the saint's most heavenly happiness is not attained in solitude, not even within the domestic circle, but where religious life exists in its social character. It was for a wider than a family circle Jesus taught us the prayer, "Our Father which art in heaven." How sweetly these words sound, when they rise in morning or evening orisons from a loving family! How impressive that prayer appears when, beneath the roof of some noble temple, a great congregation, embracing sovereign and subjects, titled peer and humble peasant, rich and poor, the lowly and the lofty, all on their knees, and with one voice uttering the words, acknowledge in men a common brotherhood, and in God a common Father! And yet that sublime invocation, "Our Father which art in heaven," will never be offered in its full sublimity till the swarthy Negro, and the roving Indian, and the wandering Tartar, and the homeless Jew, and all the pale and dark-faced tribes of men, send it up swelling to the ear of God, like the voice of many waters and the voice of mighty thunderings. Then shall a free and glad world know the tenderness, the breadth and the length of the expression, "Our Father which art in heaven."

In presenting heaven itself to us under the emblem of a city, the Bible bestows the palm, and pronounces the highest possible eulogium on city life. "There are many mansions," says our Lord, "in my Father's house." "And I," says John, "saw the holy city, New Jerusalem, coming down from God out of heaven, prepared as a bride adorned for her husband. And I heard a great voice out of heaven, saying, Behold the tabernacle of God is with men, and He will dwell with them, and they shall be his people, and He their God." Again, he says: "He carried me away in the Spirit to a great and high mountain, and showed me that great city, the holy Jerusalem, descending out of heaven from God, having the glory of God: and her light was like unto a stone most precious, even like a jasper stone, clear as crystal; and had a wall great and high, and had twelve gates, and at the gates twelve angels." "And the twelve gates were twelve pearls; every several gate was of one pearl: and the street of the city was pure gold, as it were transparent glass. And I saw no temple therein: for the Lord God Almighty and the Lamb are the temple of it. And the city had no need of the sun, neither of the moon, to shine in it: for the glory of God did lighten it, and the Lamb is the light thereof." Again he says: "After these things I heard a great voice of much people in heaven, saying, Halleluiah, salvation and glory and honor and power unto the Lord our God. And I heard as it were the voice of a great multitude, and as the voice of many waters, and as the voice of many thunderings, saying, Halleluiah, for the Lord God Omnipotent reigneth; let us be glad and rejoice, and give honor to Him, for the marriage of the Lamb is come, and His wife hath made herself ready."

May we all get an invitation to that marriage! Crowned and robed in white, may we all be found in the train of that heavenly bride! By virtue of the new birth may we all be freemen of a city never built with hands, nor hoary with the years of time—a city, whose inhabitants no census has numbered—a city, through whose streets rush no tides of business, nor nodding hearse creeps slowly with its burden to the tomb—a city, without griefs or graves, without sins or sorrows, without births or burials, without marriages or mournings—a city, which glories in having Jesus for its King, angels for its guards, saints for its citizens; whose walls are Salvation, and whose gates are Praise.

2dly. Let us attend to the evils of the city which call for Christian tears, and for something else than tears.

It is said, "Jesus beheld the city," and now, turning our eyes from Jerusalem, let us behold this city. Ere the heat of day has cast a misty veil upon the scene, or ten thousand household fires have polluted the transparent air, I take a stranger, to whom our city presents its beauties in all the charms of novelty, and conducting his steps to yonder rocky rampart, or some neighboring summit, I bid him look. Our ancient capital sits proudly throned upon her romantic hills. Gothic towers and Grecian temples, palace, castle, spires, domes, monuments and verdant gardens, picturesquely mingled, are spread out beneath his eye; and when rising from the waves of the neighboring ocean, that with amorous arms embraces the land, the sun blazes up to bathe all in golden light, he bursts into admiration, and pronounces the scene, as well he may, "the perfection of beauty." Wherever he sweeps his eye, he finds a point of view to claim his admiration. There seems nothing here to weep for. What rare variety of hill and hollow! What a happy combination of ancient and modern architecture! Here, two distant ages gaze at each other across the intervening valley, while there, fit ornament of a lone Highland glen, in the very heart of the city, crowned with cannon, and reverberating the roar of business, stands a craggy rock, proud emblem of our country's strength and independence. What scene so worthy of the enthusiasm with which the Jew exclaimed, as he surveyed Jerusalem from the top of Olivet:—"Beautiful for situation, the joy of the whole earth is Mount Zion."

But let our stranger be a man of piety as well as a man of taste, and he will love the city for its Sabbaths, more than for its scenery. No loud street cries, nor wheels of business or of pleasure, harshly grinding on holy ears, disturb the peace of the hallowed morning, or scare thoughts of heaven from his pillow. If music awakes him, it is the song of birds that from neighboring gardens call the sleeping city to arise, and join with nature in the praises of her God. A serene silence fills the street, and leaves him to hear the footfall of a solitary passenger on the unfrequented pavement. The morning meal and worship over, the chime of Sabbath bells bursts upon his ear, accompanied with the tread of many feet outside. He leaves the house with us to seek the house of God. An hour ago these streets were empty, but now such throngs are crowding them as neither the six days' business nor pleasure calls forth. Decency sits upon all faces; devoutness upon many. Laughing childhood looks unusually grave, and curbing in its playful spirit, walks with a thoughtful air. No rude manners, no laughter that bespeaks the vacant mind, no gay conversation disturbs the ear, or ill accords with the aspect of a people who look as if they were bent on some lofty purpose—to be engaged in some solemn yet not unhappy work. Their faces give the lie to a common scandal. They look serious, but not sour—they wear an air of gravity, but not of gloom. Imagine that our stranger has come from a land—from a city, such as Paris, for instance—where it may be said of the door of the church, as of the "strait gate," "few there be that find it;" where Sabbath bells are drowned in the roar of business, where labor only leaves the streets to give place to gaiety, and make room for the dance of pleasure; where the workman lays down his tools, and the merchant locks his door to whirl away the evening in Sunday ball-rooms, or applaud in the crowded theatre. With what astonishment he gazes on the crowd. Onward it sweeps, by the closed doors and windows of every place of business, to discharge itself by different streams into more than a hundred churches, and leave the thoroughfares to resume the aspect of a "deserted city," until the close of holy services again pours forth the living tide—all setting homewards, many, we trust, heavenwards.

Such is the scene our city presents on Sabbath days. Long may it continue. Beholding the city thus, our stranger sees nothing to deplore. On the contrary, as David in his exile envied the swallow which had her nest by the altar, and could fly on joyous wing at all times into the house of God, he envies us our Scottish Sabbaths, and land of precious privileges. Of a city where God is so honored, his day is so hallowed, his temples are so thronged, he is ready to say, "The Lord hath chosen Zion, he hath desired it for his habitation. This is my rest for ever; here will I dwell."

Such is the aspect in which the city may be presented. But, like the famed shield, which, because they saw it from opposite sides, one man asserted to be made of silver, and another of inferior metal, it presents two widely different aspects. Let us turn it round, and look on the other side.

I know, and I bless God for it, that there is much good, that there is a more than ordinary proportion of godly people within our walls. No sojourner has to tremble here, as Abraham did in Gerar, saying, "Surely the fear of God is not in this place." I will venture to say that no city of its population and extent contains more, few, indeed, so many, of those who are the light of the world, and the salt of the earth. In no large city, perhaps, is the Sabbath so well observed, and will there be found such a proportion of the people in the regular habit of attending a house of God. If the number of our churches may be taken as a test of piety, if the number of our hospitals and asylums may be taken as a guage of benevolence, if the number of our schools and colleges may be taken as a standard of intelligence, then, more than for its romantic beauty and picturesque position, it bears away the palm from all rival capitals, and sits enthroned and unchallenged as " Queen of Cities." Now I know all that. Yet, as there are scenes in nature where sylvan beauty is associated with features of a stern and savage character, as I have seen a lovely lake, with its gems of islands, lie sleeping under the shadow, while the woodbine, and holly, and evergreen ivy clothed the feet of a mountain which was rent into gloomy gorges, and reared its thunder-riven, naked peaks into the sky, there is much that is vicious amid all the grace, and much that is impious amid all the piety of our city. If that is true of this city, let the public be assured that it is no less true of every large city in the kingdom. Which of them shall say to us, " Stand aside, I am holier than thou?"

I once heard a venerable minister, when he came in the course of his public prayers to ask the blessing of heaven upon our town, pray that God would have mercy upon this great and wicked city. Now I can fancy that the stranger whom we have conducted through its streets on the Sabbath, and who has only mingled in its serious and most select society, would listen with astonishment to such an account of us, either from the pulpit or anywhere else. It gave offence, deep offence, to some who were proud of their native place. Yet, whether the charge excite surprise or offence, this is a wicked as well as a great city. And he heals "the hurt of the daughter of God's people slightly," he is "a dumb dog that cannot bark," who conceals that fact from either himself or others.

Under a fair and beautiful exterior, there is an extent of corruption, vile corruption, loathsome corruption, which has only to be laid bare to astonish all, and, I believe, to sicken many. Propriety forbids details. Ordinary modesty, not to say sensitive delicacy, would shrink from them. Otherwise I could raise a curtain, I could reveal that which would make your hair stand on end. Well may godly parents tremble for the virtue of their children, and every holy mother, taking alarm, gather them beneath her wings, as the moor bird does her helpless brood when hawks are screaming in the sky. I tell you who are parents, you who are the guardians of youth, that you have more need to keep an eye on the company and hours of your children, than look to the bolts and bars you trust to for protection against housebreakers and midnight-robbers. We have heard much of these. Alive to what affects the security of their property, the public have been seized with alarm, and houses, if not streets, are barricaded. But there is more in peril than your gold and silver. There is something better worth guarding, and more needing to be guarded, than anything which iron-barred shutters can secure, or watchmen protect. There are more dangerous characters than robbers prowling about our town, and walking unchallenged on our streets—permitted by our laws to do what they dare not in Paris or Berlin, to pursue their infamous occupation with barefaced, and shameless, and bold effrontery. The sword, which should be a terror to evil-doers, rusts in its sheath. And when vice is allowed so to parade our streets as to interfere with the freedom of virtuous families, and so to establish herself among us, as, by creating the worst of all nuisances, to destroy the property of a neighborhood, surely the substance of liberty is sacrificed to its shadow, and the evildoer protected at the expense of the good.

Some of us are about to make a new effort for the reclamation of fallen woman, and the protection of such as are willing, Magdalene-like, to bathe Christ's feet with tears, and wash away their deep sins in his blood. As a preliminary step to this Christian enterprise, we have procured accurate statistics of the extent of this great sin and sorrow of our large cities. Of them, I will say nothing more than this, that, while they were read, men held down their heads with shame, or held up their hands in horror, or burst out into expressions of deep indignation.

By that ravening wolf that wastes our folds, I had seen one and another, and another, and another lamb plucked out of this very flock. I had seen the once fair and promising flowers that I had cultivated in this very garden cast forth, and, as vilest weeds, trodden in the mire of the public streets. I had seen the fall of a daughter—that bitterest of domestic miseries—blanch a mother's head, and, still more terrible to look on, turn a father's heart into stone. I had known how a mother, when we all were sleeping in peace, with weary foot and weeping eyes, had gone, Christ-like, up and down these streets—searching many a den of sin to seek and save her lost one. I had seen enough to make a man exclaim, with Jeremiah, "O! that mine eyes were tears, and mine head a fountain of waters, that I might weep day and night for the daughter of my people!" But never, never had we so much as fancied the extent and horrors of this evil, the number of short-lived victims it devours, the bold daring with which the accursed trade is pursued, the invisible nets that are spread across the path of unsuspecting innocence, the fiendishly-ingenious methods which are plied to snare virtue, what masks of friendship are worn, what cunning arts of apparent kindness resorted to that vice may get the victims within her grasp, and drag them down to hell! I do believe that were the villainy and iniquity that are working and festering here and elsewhere—in every such large city—laid bare before the eyes of public virtue, nothing would restrain its indignation. Men would take the law into their own hands. Men would be a law unto themselves; and by what many might condemn as illegal, but others would applaud as a virtuous outbreak, they would sweep our cities clean of these panderers of vice, and dens of iniquity.

It is not of property, but of virtue, that families are plundered. It is not life, but souls, that are murdered among us. Crimes are done that to my eye cast into the shade the guilt of him who, having through a trade of murder supplied *subjects* for the dissecting-room, was received on the scaffold by the roar of a maddened crowd, and launched into eternity amid shouts of public indignation. That old legend of a monster, to satisfy whose voracious appetite a city had year by year to sacrifice a number of its virgins, who, amid the lamentations of their mothers and the grief of their kindred, were led away trembling to his bloody den, is no fable here. That monster is amongst us. And if there is no other way of calling forth some champions to do him battle, of rousing the public from their supineness, of stirring up the minister in the pulpit to draw the sword of the Spirit, and the magistrate on the bench to draw the sword of the state, it may be necessary to throw this report out of its present secresy, and leave it to burst upon the city like a shell.

I am guilty of no exaggeration. I ask you, meanwhile, to believe that—and that, with all our apparent goodness, there lies beneath the surface much which no Christian man could behold, without—like our pure and pitiful

Saviour—weeping over it. I know enough to call upon the young to shun the associate, who is infected with vice, more than the one infected with plague or deadly fever. Keep away from them that are going down to hell, more than from the grasp of a drowning man. "My son, hear the instruction of thy father, and forsake not the law of thy mother." "If sinners entice thee, consent thou not." "Keep thy heart with all diligence." "Ponder the path of thy feet," that they may never follow one of whom it is written—"Her feet go down to death, her steps take hold on hell."

I also know enough to implore parents, most prayerfully, to commit their children to the keeping of an all-present God. Guard them sedulously. Fold them early. Before the night brings out the ravenous wolf, and the wily fox, and the roaring lion, have all your lambs at home. Make it a bright, cheerful home. Mingle firmness with kindness. And from late hours, from dangerous companions, from nightly scenes of pleasure and amusement, more carefully keep your children than you bolt door or window against those, who can but plunder your house of property, that is of infinitely less value than your domestic purity, of jewels, infinitely less precious than your children's souls.

SERMON II.

"He beheld the city, and wept over it."—LUKE xix. 41.

WITHOUT driver, without hand to curb or guide him, a startled, maddened horse, with snowy foam speckling his mane, and the fire flashing from his heels, was once seen tearing along through a country village. He dragged a cart behind him. A little child was in it, who, every moment in danger of being dashed upon the road, clung to its sides in pale terror. A woman, as it passed, shot from her doorway, like an arrow from the bow-string. With outstretched arms, dishevelled hair, and flying feet, she followed in full pursuit, filling the street with cries—that might have pierced a heart of stone—"Save that child; save that child!" Whereupon a man, who had not humanity enough to join the chase and swell the cry, far less bravery enough, at his own peril, to throw himself across the path and seize the reins, coolly turned round on her to bid her cease her cries, saying, "Woman, it is not your child." The information was not new to her. She had left all her own safe in their nest at home. Nor did that heartless speech for a moment arrest her step, or still the cry of "Save that child; save that child!"

In that circumstance we have more than a touching example of the tenderness of a woman's heart. It illustrates the spirit of the gospel. A noble and generous woman! She was imbued with the large loving-heartedness that is unhappy if others are miserable, that will not eat its own bread and drink its own cup alone, that is not content to be safe without also saving. There, in these outstretched arms, that anxious cry, those feet that hasten to save, you see, standing out in beautiful contrast to selfishness, the broad, wide, warm benevolence of the gospel, the spirit of Calvary, the mind that was in Jesus Christ—and which, let me add, is in all that are Jesus

Christ's. This furnishes a touchstone for testing a religious profession.

A man, I pray you to observe, may be a true Christian, who falls even into grievous sin. Many a bark with sprung masts, and torn sails, and shattered bulwarks, gains the port. And many a man gets to heaven who has been all but wrecked. Indeed, "the righteous scarcely are saved," and the vessel which has her head laid heavenward, keeping careless watch, and thrown, so to speak, on her beam ends, by some sudden gust of temptation, may all but founder. In Bible story, as well as other records of Christian experience, how many solemn warnings have we to watch and pray; how much that rolls out the loud alarum, "Let him that thinketh he standeth take heed lest he fall." We do not say that a Christian man cannot fall into sin. Yet it is one thing to fall into sin, it is another to lie in it, to love it, to seek it, to court it, to pursue it, to enjoy it—as it is pursued and enjoyed by those who, in place of rejecting it, "like gravel in the mouth," "roll it as a sweet morsel under their tongue." It is one thing, being overcome of evil, to be the devil's captive—bewitched, beguiled, caught in a snare and cast into darkness—and another to be a base deserter, a bold soldier, fighting in the ranks of Satan.

Far be it from me to excuse or even palliate those sins in good men which crucify the Lord afresh, and inflict the deepest wounds upon his bleeding side. Yet the sin, which has set loose many a ribald tongue, which they "tell in Gath, and publish in the streets of Askelon," which fills the church with grief, and makes the world ring with scandal, which, as when some shot in battle dismounts a cannon, or explodes a magazine, or cuts down a man of mark, is hailed by the enemy with shouts of triumph, even such a sin may say less against a man's piety, than the love that embraces the lost, and a deep interest in the best welfare of others, say for it. Look at Noah beneath the mantle which filial piety has flung over him. Look at Peter denying his master. Look at the saintly David covered with blushes and confusion, and cowering under the fixed and eagle eye of him, who points his finger, saying, "Thou art the man!" Such scenes, even such scenes in a man's life, do not present an aspect of character incompatible with a true and genuine piety. But such an aspect is presented by many a decent man who never brought a scandal on religion, yet never beheld the city to weep over it, never spent one anxious thought on any interests but his own, never spared a tear for any losses but his own, never, so be that his own nest was warmly feathered, troubled himself about others' wants, nor cared what came of them, if he accomplished his own selfish ends. The sins of a good man are but the diseases of life—the irregular palpitations of a living heart; but that cold indifference, that unfeeling selfishness—these are the rigidity and frigidity of death.

I remember a remark which once dropped from the lips of an aged minister. The subject of his discourse was our Lord's last sufferings. And when he narrated how they had brought him to Calvary and nailed him on the tree, and was telling how the impenitent thief turned on his cross—a dying man to mock a dying Saviour—he stopped to remark, that while there was almost no sin which a child of God might not fall into, there was one thing which he had never read of a good man doing, and which he believed no good man had ever done or would do—he would never sit in the scorner's chair, nor make a mock of piety. And another such test of real religion this subject presents. It may also be employed to prove the truth or falsehood of our profession. I venture to affirm, that however great his faults may be, no man of God, no man animated by the spirit of Jesus Christ, no child baptized into the nature as well as name of that heavenly Father, who is unwilling that any should perish—no man allied to those angelic beings, who minister to suffering saints, and rejoice in the conversion of the lowest of the lost—no man imbued with the love which, to save the most wicked, most worthless, and most wretched of us, left the Father's bosom to hang in infancy on a woman's breast, and hang in death on a bloody tree—will refuse to lend me a willing ear, when I lay open the sores and sorrows, and plead for the souls of men. Of too many this may be true :—"They lie upon beds of ivory, and stretch themselves upon their couches, and eat the lambs out of the flock, and the calves out of the midst of the stall; they chant to the sound of the viol, and invent to themselves instruments of music, like David; they drink wine in bowls, and anoint themselves with the chief ointments, but they are not grieved for the affliction of Joseph." But I cast myself with confidence upon God's people. I resume my subject, and proceed to set forth the sins and sorrows of our cities—fully assured that I shall not meet from lips which the altar-coal has touched, the words with which the murderers of our Lord thrust forth the traitor—" What is that to us? See thou to that."

II. The intemperance of the city—or, to use a plainer term, to call things by their right names, to be done with sacrificing men's souls and public morals to a spurious delicacy, to make vice as disgusting and detestable as possible, to rub off the paint that conceals the rotten cheek, let me say, in plain broad Saxon, its *Drunkenness.*

Our subject is one for the pulpit. From preachers it claims more notice and warning, more plain denunciation and earnest pleading, than, perhaps, it usually receives. Some might be better pleased were I, instead of conducting them through loathsome scenes, to be their guide into the temple—to show them, in succession, the sublime mysteries of our faith. But what saith the Lord: "Son of Man, I have set thee a watchman unto the house of Israel, therefore thou shalt hear the word from my mouth, and warn them from me. When I say unto the wicked man, Thou shalt surely die, if thou dost not speak to warn the wicked man from his way, that wicked man shall die in his iniquity, but his blood will I require at thine hand." Again, what saith the Lord: "Set the trumpet to thy mouth. Blow ye the trumpet in Zion, and sound an alarm in my holy mountain." Are people concerned for the honor of the temple? How can they so well express this feeling as by attempting with Jesus to purify its courts? Is the Lord, as some think, coming? Let us go forth, like John Baptist—forerunners to prepare his way. Have we asked of them who keep ward and watch on the towers of Zion, "Watchman, what of the night? Watchman, what of the night?" and got back the startling answer, "The morning cometh and also the night?" The more need have we to abandon all airy speculation, and betake ourselves to the practical work of setting heart and house, town and country, church and state in order. Let us all get ready, and get all things ready for Christ's second coming. Laying aside the telescopes which we had turned in the expected direction, let us gird up our loins, go down into the field of work, make straight what is crooked, and smooth what is rough, and, preparing his way, remove whatever would offend the eye of our coming King.

The apostles were not content to preach only what are called doctrinal discourses. In the texture both of their sermons and epistles, they wove up doctrine and duty together. These were mingled as the woof and warp of that loom, where the flying shuttle weaves the sail with which men catch the winds of heaven, and impel the bark onwards to her desired haven. We see these inspired preachers coming down to the common business and practical duties of life—down from the throne of God—from the heights of the cross—from regions of such high speculation, that Peter owns himself to have lost sight of Paul, just as in summer day, when watching the lark as she rose from the dewy grass, we have seen her mount up on untiring wing, till she became a mere dark speck upon the blue sky, and then, although her song still came ringing down, vanished from our field of vision. From heights so lofty the men, who were moved by the Holy Ghost, descended to expatiate on the most common topics that belong to practical piety. They taught masters how to rule, and servants how to work. They taught husbands how to love, and children how to obey. They laid down rules for a bishop's table. They no more thought it beneath their dignity to tell young women how to attire their heads and dress their hair, than to warn young men to "flee youthful lusts." They lifted up their warning against the sins of ordinary life. They raised beacons on every quicksand and sunken rock. They buoyed out the channel of salvation. Describing with downright plainness those fruits of the flesh which exclude from the kingdom, they did not sacrifice God's truth, human virtue, and precious souls upon the altar of a false and spurious delicacy. They went in among corruption, like the sunbeam which shows it, but suffers no taint through the contact. Descending from the loftiest to the lowliest subjects, theirs was the course of the eagle, which, now on cloud-cleaving wing, mounts upwards—soaring out of sight—and now sweeps down to brush the heather, or settle in her rocky nest. Overleaping all the laws of spurious delicacy, theirs was the noble spirit of the Roman. Men placed him at the bar of his country. They charged him with a violation of her laws. Fresh from the fight, covered with the blood of a battle-field where he had led his country's armies to victory, he replied, "I have broken the law, but I have saved the state." And could I, by God's blessing, save a sinner, could I pluck some perishing one from ruin, could I successfully warn that young man or young woman who, all unconscious of their danger, are drawing near the brink of destruction, I would throw delicacy to the winds, saying, I have broken its laws, but I have saved a soul.

With what plainness of speech did Paul warn! with what truth and tenderness did he plead! He looks on sinners as a trembling mother on her rash boy, when hanging half way over some beetling cliff, he stretches down his hand to pluck from the rock its wild and withering flowers. "As my beloved sons," Paul cries, "I warn you." He exhorts Timothy to rebuke "in season and out of season." He eschews those general denunciations of sin that are as little felt as general confessions of it are; that, like things with broad blunt points, neither pierce the skin nor penetrate the sore. The apostle enters into particulars. One by one, name by name, sin by sin, he writes out, on several occasions, the long black catalogue of prevailing vices. And in these, as if, like the poisoned garment that stuck to Hercules, it could not be plucked from the body of humanity, this vice of drunkenness—the sin, the shame, the weakness of our nation—finds a never failing and prominent place. It is the weakness as well as sin and shame of our nation. The world knows that. Other nations taunt us with that. Nor do scenes at home allow me to forget the strange but stinging remark of a foreigner who said, "It is a blessed thing for the world that you Anglo-Saxons are a drunken race. Such are your powers, and energy, and talent, that otherwise you would have become masters of the world!" So much for taking up the subject. Now let us look—

1. *To the extent of this vice.*

First, *In our country.* No good cause has ever but suffered from injudicious zeal and extravagant statements. Regard for truth and my very anxiety to see this evil arrested, unite in preventing me from indulging in exaggeration—were it possible here to exaggerate. I say possible to exaggerate; for what flight of fancy, what bold strokes of painting, what graphic powers of description, could convey any adequate idea of the evils and sorrows that march in the train of this direful, and most detestable vice? Standing on the surf-beaten shore, when ocean, lashed by the tempest into foaming rage, was up in her angry might, I have seen a spectacle so grand; and where she couched in the valley, arrayed in a gay robe of summer flowers, I have seen nature so beautiful; and where rattling thunders mingled with the roar of the avalanche, while high above the dark mysterious gorge, within which the battle of elements was waging, rose clear and serene untrodden peaks of eternal snow, I have looked upon scenes so sublime, as to pass description. Nor color nor words can convey an adequate idea of them. To be understood they must be visited, to be felt they must be seen.

Incredible as it may appear, this remark is no less true of many regions of sorrow, and starvation, and disease, and vice, and devilry, and death, that the smoke-stained walls of these dingy houses hide from common view. These formed for years the painful field of my labors. Let no man fancy that we select the worst cases, that we present the worst side of the picture before them. Believe me, it is impossible to exaggerate, impossible even truthfully to paint the effect of this vice either on those who are addicted to it, or those who suffer from it—crushed husbands, broken-hearted wives, and most of all, those poor innocent children that are dying under cruelty and starvation, that shiver in their rags upon our streets, that walk the winter snows with naked feet, and with their matted hair, and hollow cheeks, and sunken eyes, and sallow countenances, glare out on us, wild and savage-like, from these patched and dusty windows. Besides, if the extent of this evil has been exaggerated, it is a fault that may be pardoned. It is a failing that "leans to virtue's side." Perhaps she exaggerates his danger, but who quarrels with the mother, whose affection for her sailor boy keeps her tossing on a sleepless pillow, praying through the long hours of a stormy night, as her busy imagination fancies that in that wild shriek of the fitful wind she hears his drowning cry? When the nursery only has caught fire, and a faithful domestic, plucking the babe from a burning cradle, rushes into your chamber, and makes you leap to the cry—the house is all on fire; will he, that hurries away to save the rest, challenge the exaggeration? It is as natural to earnestness of purpose and depth of feeling, as a blush to shame, or a smile to happiness, or the flash of the eye to anger.

I admit, indeed I assert, that, in regard to

our own division of the island, the extent of this evil has been exaggerated. Not many years ago, a distinguished patriot rose in the Commons' House of Parliament, and mourning over his fatherland—for he had drawn his first breath on this side of the Border—declared that Scotland was the most drunken country, and the Scotch the most drunken nation on the face of the earth. I am well aware that with all the superior privileges which are our boast, we cannot hold up an unabashed and unblushing face before France, or Germany, or Switzerland. In the course of last summer, I spent seven weeks in these countries. I saw Paris at a time of national rejoicing, the population of that gay city all let loose from business to pursue pleasure at their will. If in that mighty crowd there were gloomy looks turned on the royal pomp and serried regiments that conducted to his baptism the infant heir of a throne, which, unlike our Queen's, firmly based on the affections of the people, sits unsteadily on the rim of the wheel of fortune, the eye detected no drunkard. If some were sullen, all were sober; and that feature characterized also those dangerous quarters of the city, where the lowest classes resided, where rebellions had been hatched, and volcanic revolutions had burst forth—burying throne and altars in a common ruin. I was also in Brussels during three days of prolonged public fêtes. All its people were abroad in the streets, and the throng was swelled by some fifty thousand who had poured into the capital from the various cities of the kingdom. Yet, in these different kingdoms, neither in their mountain hamlets, nor crowded cities, were there presented so many cases of intemperance in these seven weeks, as may be seen almost any day in Edinburgh, or other large city of our island, in seven short hours.

Yet it is not true that Scotland is the most drunken country in the world. This is a misstatement. As a lover of my country, I am anxious to deny it, and still more anxious to deny it, because I see that men have taken occasion from it to sneer at our religion.

They allege, that our strict observance of the Sabbath is the cause of our intemperance. They say, that if we would sanction public amusements, and open our theatres on the Lord's day, we would check this evil, and nurse our people up in habits of sobriety. Much as I value them, I would not defend our Sabbath observances at the expense of truth. I would not blacken other countries to make my own look fair. But the statement is not consistent with fact. The Lapland mother pours strong brandy over the throat of her sucking child. In the northern parts of Europe, among the nations who inhabit its colder regions, deep drinking is as rife as it is here. Shall we cross the channel? In Ireland I saw more well-to-do-like men and women leaving a market town on an ordinary market day with unsteady step, than I ever saw on a similar occasion on this side the Irish channel. Shall we cross the Border? During occasional visits to London, I have seen drunkenness on a scale far more gigantic than during a residence of twenty years, I ever saw it in the lowest districts of this city. In the charges of the English judges, who has not read how they attribute almost all the crimes of their country, directly or indirectly, to the baneful influences of drink? I have been present in England's high courts of justice, and when panel succeeded panel at the bar, the course of the trials brought out the fact, that the beer-shops were in almost every case connected with the crimes.

This false charge, let me remark, has arisen from circumstances, which are rather creditable to us than otherwise. I will explain that. There is a city in England, which contains a larger population than our own; and yet it appeared from the police reports that it presented three times fewer cases of drunkenness. This seemed to crown them with glory, and cover us with shame. But upon farther inquiry, we found that they had no right to the laurel. There the police conduct the drunkard home, and thus his case does not appear upon record; here, on the other hand, regarded as a public nuisance, deserving no such gentle treatment, he is conducted to the police office, and so gets his case entered in our statistics of crime. Thus, as you will see, our superior strictness made us, as compared with some other cities, appear worse than we really were. Such also has been the effect of our very efforts boldly to expose this evil; with God's blessing resolutely to arrest its progress. Thanks especially to our temperance societies, they have thrown a flood of daylight upon the subject. And be it remembered, that the chamber of him, who has opened the shutters, and let in the sunbeams, and is busy sweeping cobwebs from the wall and dust from the floor, foul as it seems, may be less so than a room more unused to brooms and less fully illuminated with the light of day. We have brought out the evil. We have dragged the monster from his den, for all the world to gaze at him, and hate him, and kill him, if they can.

In standing up for my country, in stating what I believe to be nothing more or less than the truth, where or when, let me ask, did our

Scottish Sabbaths ever present such scenes as those that follow? They appear in evidence given before a committee of the House of Commons. Horrible illustrations of what our religion and country have to suffer from this crime, it is painful, it is loathsome, to read them. Yet he who would cure disease, and save from death, must nerve himself to endure the horrors of the dissecting-room.

A member of the vestry, and a governor of the poor, in the parish of St. Margarets, was asked whether the increase in the number of drinkers had increased beyond the number of the inhabitants. He replies, "Yes; and I think the character of the drinkers has deteriorated! Last Sunday morning, I arose about seven o'clock, and looked from my bed-room at the gin-palace opposite to me. I saw it surrounded with customers; amongst them I saw two coal porters, apparently with women who appeared to be their wives, and a little child, about six or seven years old. These forced their way through the crowd after much struggling; they got to the bar, and came out again in a short time, one of the women so intoxicated as to be unable to walk; she went against the door-post, and then fell flat on the pavement, with her legs partly in the shop. The three who were with her, attempted to raise her, but they were so intoxicated as to be unable to perform that task; their efforts to perform that were ludicrous, and the doors were opened wide into the shop to admit of the ingress and egress of customers, who passed by laughing at that which appeared to them a most comic scene. After a considerable time they succeeded in raising the woman, but she fell again; they then brought her to the side, and placed her against the door-post, and there she sat, with her head in her bosom, apparently insensible; the little child who was with her came and endeavored to arouse her, by smacking her on the legs and on the body, and on the face, but she appeared quite insensible; the little thing appeared to be the most sensible of the party. During this time, a woman almost in a state of nudity, with a fine infant at her breast, the only dress being its night shirt, followed by another child about eight years old, an interesting little girl, naked, except a night-shirt, and without either shoes or stockings, followed a wretched looking man into the house, and remained there some time. I saw them struggling through the crowd to get to the bar. They all had their gin; the infant had the first share from the woman's glass; they came back to the outside of the door, and there could hardly stand, but appeared ripe for quarrel. The little child in her arms cried, and the wretched woman beat it most unmercifully."

He states also:—"Last Sunday morning I had occasion to walk through the Broadway a few minutes before eleven o'clock. I found the pavement before every gin-shop crowded; just as church-time approached, the gin-shops sent forth their multitudes, swearing, and fighting, and bawling obscenely; some were stretched on the pavement, insensibly drunk, while every few steps the foot-way was taken up by drunken wretches being dragged to the station-house by the police."

The same witness was asked:—Has the habit of drinking among women much increased, so far as your observation extends? He answers:—"I think it has extended, and the children appear to be initiated to the drinking of spirits from their infancy;" and he calls the special attention of the Committee to the fact, "that the poor wretched girls who live by prostitution, and who are the best customers to the gin-shops, die off in about four years." Now mark how that brief course of vice and its terrible end stand out in contrast to the unholy gains of those who feed its fires. This witness states, that, in three gin-shops close by him, "more than twenty thousand pounds is year by year taken for spirits consumed upon the premises; and that within a circle containing a population of 40,000 people, not less than £50,000 is expended on gin alone!" Oh, if that is a frightful vice which eats, like a cancer, into a woman's breast, that is a frightful trade, which, fungus-like, lives upon the corruption of human nature—the decay of our noblest faculties, the death of our best affections. He is, for himself, a wretched fool, who builds up a fortune out of sin and misery. One blow of death's hand will shatter it, and what will he do when he has to confront all those who accuse him of their ruin—when he stands at the bar of God as ragged and naked as that wretched woman whom first a villain spoiled of her virtue, and threw her away, and next he plunders of her shame and money—casting her forth upon the cold, hard street.

This evidence, no doubt, was given some years ago; but with our own eyes we have seen spectacles of sin and misery in London bad as anything that witness has depicted. Let us hear no more therefore of the strict Sabbaths of Scotland driving our people into the arms of intemperance. It was the fair face of England these loathsome spectacles blotted. They were to be seen in her metropolis, under the shadow of religion's antique and venerable towers, near by the palace of royalty, and in the immediate vicinity of the halls of legislation. While our senators, fired with the ambition of old Rome, push Britain's conquests to distant lands, and flare up with indignation at the slightest insult offered to her flag, let them learn that these scenes most of all dishonor us. It is neither my pleasure, nor my part, to speak " evil of dignities ;" but having regard only to the interests of truth, of humanity, of God's glory and man's good, I will be bold to say, that unless those into whose hands we have committed the affairs of our country, cease to swell the revenues of the state out of the vices of the people, and promptly apply every possible cure to these crying evils, they will peril the existence and betray the best interests of our empire. If conquests are to be pushed abroad, while our deadliest enemies are left to make such havoc at home, our legislators will stand open to the charge of Solomon :—" The eyes of a fool are in the ends of the earth." A remark, let me add, not more applicable to the state than to the church, if in seeking to convert the heathen abroad, she forgets the heathen at home.

Secondly, *Let us look more particularly at the intemperance of our own city.*

She has no occasion to sit proudly on her hills and look down on others. We have cause to thank God for that Act of Parliament, by which, in answer to the voice of an all but unanimous people, the drinking-shops of Scotland were closed, and all traffic in intoxicating liquors pronounced illegal, from Saturday night till Monday morning. We give God thanks for that. What we gained, we intend to keep. What we won, we shall resolutely defend. We have no intention of retreating. On the contrary, we desire to see the law of the Sabbath extended to every day of the week, and all shops opened for the mere purposes of drinking shut—shut up, as a curse to the community—as carrying on a trade, not less than the opium-shops of China, incurably pernicious. The evil, which cannot be cured, condemns itself to death.

But, amid the improved aspect of our Sabbaths, we cannot forget that before the Act which I have alluded to was passed, in the more than forty thousand visits paid on the Lord's day to the drinking shops, we had a fact, terribly symptomatic of the extent and virulence of the disease. Nor can we shut our eyes to week-day scenes. You have only to walk our streets to see how this vice rages far and wide, and goes about them "like a roaring lion, seeking whom it may devour." I should be ashamed to walk some districts of this city with a native of that ancient nation with which we are now at war, and to which, God grant that we may soon be reconciled. "The wrath of man worketh not the righteousness of God;" and who would not rather see our fleets with flowing sails approach these distant shores to land a freight of merchandise, Bibles, and messengers of peace, than cannon, and serried regiments, and other armaments of war? With a pagan from any part of that vast empire, but one which our opium-trade and greed of gain had demoralized, I say that I should be afraid to find myself in many districts of this city of colleges, and churches, and hospitals, and benevolent societies, and people of high Christian worth and unquestionable piety.

Amid the idle groups of bloated women, and half-naked children, and wrecks of men, filling up almost every close-mouth and foot of filthy stair, with our path crossed by some reeling drunkard, who launches himself into the common sewer, with so many shops under Government license, turning health into disease, decency into tattered rags, love into estrangement or bitter hatred, young beauty into loathsomeness, woman's natural modesty into loud and coarse effrontery, mothers' milk into poison, mothers' hearts into stone, and the image of God into something baser than a brute; how could I look that sober, upright pagan in the face, and ask him to become a Christian? I must be dumb, lest he should turn round on me to ask:—Are these Christians? Be these the fruits of Christianity? . I would repel the ·charge. But what if he should follow it up with a blow less easy to parry? Pointing up to those here who are rolling in wealth, or enjoying the abundant comforts of their homes, or the ordinances of their worship, he might next ask:—What are these Christians doing? What do they to save their fellow-creatures from miseries that move a pagan to tears? What to save them from crimes unpractised by those whom you call the followers of the false prophet, by us to whose distant land you send your missionaries to turn us from our fathers' idols? What could I say? How would I look? With what answer could I meet the withering sarcasm:—"Physician, heal thyself?"

But let us leave the lowest class and rise into a higher region. Not that it would alter my position or abate my zeal if I believed that it was none but the lowest of the low who fell victims to this vice. They are our brethren. They shiver in the cold, and pine under hunger, as well as we. They have feelings, sensitive to wrong and pain, as well as we. They have heart-strings to be broken, as well as we. They have souls to be saved, as well as we— souls as precious and priceless as our own. A diamond is a diamond whether it lies buried in a dust heap, or flashes on beauty's finger, or is set in a golden crown. I hold a beggar's soul to be as valuable as a king's; and that he who dies in a hovel, goes on the same footing before a God in judgment, as the hero, whose death has thrown a nation into mourning, and who is borne to the tomb, through crowded streets, with the honors and parade of a public funeral.

Go not away, I pray you, under the delusion, that like a fog-bank which lies thick and heavy on the valley, when heights are clear, and hill tops are beaming in the morning sun, intemperance is confined only to the lowest stratum of society. I know the contrary. Much improved as are the habits of the upper and middle classes—and we thank God for that, extending as that improvement has done to those who stand beneath them in the social pyramid—and we bless God also for that, and hoping that this improvement, like water percolating a bed of sand, will sink down till it reaches and purifies the lowest stratum, we have met this vice in all classes of society. It has cost many a servant her place, and—still greater loss—ruined her virtue. It has broken the bread of many a tradesman. It has wrecked the fortunes of many a merchant. It has spoiled the coronet of its lustre, and sunk rank into contempt. It has sent respectability to hide its head in a poor-house, and presented scenes in luxurious drawing-rooms, which have furnished laughter to the scullions in the kitchen.

But it has done worse things than break the staff of bread, lower rank, wreck fortunes, and crown wealth with thorns. Most accursed vice! What hopes so precious that it has not withered, what career so promising that it has not arrested, what heart so tender, what temper so fine, that it has not destroyed, what things so noble and sacred that it has not blasted? Touched by its hell-fire flame the laurel crown has been changed into ashes on the head of mourning genius, and, the wings of the poet scorched by it, he who once played in the light of sun-beams and soared aloft into the skies, has basely crawled in the dust. Paralysing the mind, even more than the body, it has turned the noblest intellect into drivelling idiocy. Not awed by dignity, it has polluted the ermine of the judge. Not scared away by the sanctity of the temple, it has defiled the pulpit. In all these particulars, I speak what I know. I have seen it cover with a cloud, or expose to deposition from the office and honors of the holy ministry, no fewer than ten clergymen, with some of whom I have sat down at the table of the Lord, and all of whom I numbered in the rank of acquaintances or friends.

The frightful extent of this vice, however, is perhaps most brought out by one melancholy fact. There are few families amongst us so happy as not to have had some one near and dear to them either in imminent peril—hanging over the precipice—or the slave of intemperance, altogether "sold unto sin." Considering the depravity of human nature, and the temptations to which our customs and circumstances expose us, that fact, however melancholy and full of warning, does not astonish us. But, to see a father or mother, to see a brother or sister venturing on the edge of a whirlpool, in whose devouring, damning vortex they themselves have seen one whom they loved engulphed, does fill us with astonishment. I knew a mother once, who saw her only son drowned before her eyes. Years came and went ere she could calmly look upon the ocean, or hear without pain the roar of the billows where her boy was lost. How many have a better or rather a bitterer cause for hating the sight of the bowl! Considering how many are lost—drowned there, I do wonder that so few Christian, or no Christian, but loving parents, candidly consider the question, whether it be not their duty to train up their children according to the rule, "Taste not, touch not, handle not." I have wondered most of all to see a father indulging in the cup that had been poison, and death to his son. Why does he not throw it away—cast it from him with horror! Taking the knife, red with the blood of his child—making sure that it shall be the death of none else—why does he not fling it after the lost one—down, down into the depths of hell?

Standing amid havoc and ruins, with so many in our neighborhoods, and in our churches, whom this vice has utterly wrecked, what prayer so suitable as this:—"O God! lift up thy feet unto the perpetual desolations! Thine enemies roar in the midst of thy congregations. They break down the carved work thereof with axes and with hammers. They have cast fire into thy sanctuary. They have defiled the dwelling-place of thy name. O God! how long shall the adversary reproach? Shall the enemy blaspheme thy name for ever? Have respect unto thy covenant! The dark places of the earth are full of the habitations of horrid cruelty. Forget not the congregation of thy poor for ever. Arise, O Lord, and plead the cause that is thine own."

What, now, although the evil may have been exaggerated? It has been alleged that not less than Sixty Millions of money are spent year by year on intoxicating stimulants within the United Kingdom. Reduce the sum by one-half, let it be but Thirty, and apart altogether from the ruin it works in so many cases on all that is good, and noble, and blessed, and beautiful, and holy, how great a waste! Are there no hungry ones to feed, no naked to clothe, no orphans to adopt, no unhappy children left uncared for and untaught, no favorable outlets for our money on the heathenism of home or foreign fields? There are. And when the poor are starving, when souls are perishing, when we are straitened for want of funds to supply the gospel at home, or send missionaries to tell the heathen world of Jesus and his love, how shall we face a day of judgment—we who spend a sum equal to half the whole revenue of the British empire on what is in all cases a luxury, in most cases an injury, and in many a most fatal indulgence? Before we are summoned into the Master's presence, it is well to be thinking how we are to meet the demand, " Give an account of thy stewardship."

Again, it has been stated, that through the

direct and indirect effects produced by these stimulants, Sixty thousand lives are annually lost. Reduce that also by one-half, and what a quotient remains! Thirty thousand human lives offered in annual sacrifice at the bloody shrine of this idol! Death is bitter enough in any circumstances to the bereaved. However precious our comforts be, all memory of the dead is more or less painful. We put out of sight the toys of the little hands that are mouldering in the silent grave. The picture of the dear one, whose eyes our fingers have closed, and whose face the shroud has covered, hangs veiled upon the wall. The remembrance of the loved and lost will throw on life's brightest scenes the cold shadow of a cloud, which discharges its burden of grief sometimes in a few drops, sometimes in a shower of tears. But over how many of these thirty thousand deaths is there the mourning that has no hope! What incurable wounds have they inflicted! What sad memories have they left! They talk of war! What is war to that? Give me her bloody bed, bury me or mine in a soldier's rather than in a drunkard's grave! Innocent children, killed off by cold and hunger, slowly starved to death—coffins that hold broken hearts—woman's remorse for her virtue lost, gnawing like a vulture at life's quivering vitals—poor, pitiable wretches, with palsied hands and shrivelled limbs, in loop-holed poverty, who would give the world to be able, as in better and bygone days, to love their wives and bless their children, and enjoy the esteem of their neighbors, sinking into death by inches, or staggering at a sudden call up to the bar of judgment! Thirty thousand such cases, year by year, in this kingdom! Than that, give me rather the battle-field. With a good cause to fight for, and bugles sounding the assault, give me the red rush of gallent men who dash across the lines of death, and leaping in at every breach and embrasure, strike for the liberties of man—falling with their mother's Bible in their breast, a mother's and Jesus' name mingled on their dying lips! "No drunkard shall inherit the kingdom of God." But of those who sleep in Jesus, whether they died with gentle and holy voices in their ear, or amid the crash of musketry and roar of canon—"I heard a voice from heaven, saying unto me, Write, Blessed are the dead which die in the Lord, from henceforth, yea, saith the Spirit, that they may rest from their labors, and their works do follow them."

SERMON III.

"When he beheld the city, he wept over it."—LUKE xix. 41.

THERE is a remarkable phenomenon to be seen on certain parts of our own coast. Strange to say, it proves, notwithstanding such expressions as the stable and solid land, that it is not the land but the sea which is the stable element. On some summer day, when there is not a wave to rock her, nor breath of wind to fill her sail or fan a cheek, you launch your boat upon the waters, and, pulling out beyond lowest tide mark, you idly lie upon her bows to catch the silvery glance of a passing fish, or watch the movements of the many curious creatures that travel the sea's sandy bed, or, creeping out of their rocky homes, wander its tangled mazes. If the traveller is surprised to find a deep-sea shell embedded in the marbles of a mountain peak, how great is your surprise to see beneath you a vegetation foreign to the deep! Below your boat, submerged many feet beneath the surface of the lowest tide, away down in these green crystal depths, you see no rusting anchor, no mouldering remains of some shipwrecked one, but in the standing stumps of trees you discover the mouldering vestiges of a forest, where once the wild cat prowled, and the birds of heaven, singing their loves, had nestled and nursed their young. In counterpart to those portions of our coast where sea-hollowed caves, with sides the waves have polished, and floors still strewed with shells and sand, now stand high above the level of the strongest stream-tides, there stand these dead decaying trees—entombed in the deep. A strange phenomenon, which admits of no other explanation, than this, that there the coast line has sunk beneath its ancient level.

Many of our cities present a phenomenon as melancholy to the eye of a philanthropist, as the other is interesting to a philosopher, or geologist. In their economical, educational, moral, and religious aspects, certain parts of this city bear palpable evidence of a corresponding subsidence. Not a single house, nor a block of houses, but whole streets, once from end to end the abodes of decency, and industry, and wealth, and rank, and piety, have been engulphed. A flood of ignorance, and misery, and sin, now breaks and roars above the top of their highest tenements. Nor do the old stumps of a forest, still standing up erect beneath the sea-wave, indicate a greater change, a deeper subsidence, than the relics of ancient grandeur, and the touching memorials of piety which yet linger about these wretched dwellings, like evening twilight on the hills—like some traces of beauty on a corpse. The unfurnished floor, the begrimed and naked walls, the stifling, sickening atmosphere, the patched and dusty window--through which a sunbeam, like hope, is faintly stealing, the ragged, hunger-bitten, and sad-faced children, the ruffian man, the heap of straw where some wretched mother, in muttering dreams, sleeps off last night's debauch, or lies unshrouded and uncoffined in the ghastliness of a hopeless death, are sad scenes. We have often looked on them. And they appear all the sadder for the restless play of fancy. Excited by some vestiges of a fresco-painting that still looks out from the foul and broken plaster, the massive marble rising over the cold and cracked hearth-stone, an elaborately carved cornice too high for shivering cold to pull it down for fuel, some stucco flowers or fruit yet pendant on the crumbling ceiling, fancy, kindled by these, calls up the scenes and actors of other days—when beauty, elegance, and fashion graced these lonely halls, and plenty smoked on groaning tables, and where these few cinders, gathered from the city dust-heap, are feebly smouldering, hospitable fires roared up the chimney.

But there is that in and about these houses which bears witness of a deeper subsidence, a yet sadder change. Bent on some mission of mercy, you stand at the foot of a dank and filthy stair. It conducts you to the crowded rooms of a tenement, where—with the exception of some old decent widow who has seen better days, and when her family are all dead, and her friends are all gone, still clings to God and her faith in the dark hour of adversity and amid the wreck of fortune—from the cellar-dens below to the garrets beneath the roof-tree, you shall find none either reading their Bible, or even with a Bible to read. Alas! of prayer, of morning and evening psalms, of earthly or heavenly peace, it may be said that the place that once knew them, knows them no more. But before you enter thee door-way, raise your eyes to the stone above it. Dumb, it speaks of other and better times. Carved in Greek or Latin, or our own mother tongue, you decipher such texts as these:—" Peace be to this house." "Except the Lord build the house, they labor in vain that build it." " We have a building of God, an house not made with hands eternal in the heavens." "Fear God;" or this, "Love your neighbor." Like the mouldering remnants of a forest that once resounded with the melody of birds, but hears nought now save the angry dash or melancholy moan of breaking waves, these vestiges of piety furnish a guage which enables us to measure how low in these dark localities the whole stratum of society has sunk.

Now there are forces in nature which, heaving up the crust of our earth, may convert the sea bed again into forest or corn land. At this moment these forces are in active operation. Working slowly, yet with prodigious power, they are now raising the coasts of Sweden in the old world and of Chili in the new. And who knows but these subterranean agencies, elevating our own coasts, may yet restore verdure to those deep sea sands—giving back to the plough its soil, to waving pines their forest land. And thus on our shores, redeemed from the grasp of the ocean in some future era, golden harvests may fall to the reaper's song, and tall forests to the woodman's axe. We know not whether this shall happen. But I do know that there is a force at work in this world—gentle, yet powerful—commonly slow in action, but always sure in its results, which, mightier than volcanic fires, pent-up vapor, or rocking earthquake, is adequate to raise the most sunken masses of society, and restore the lowest and longest neglected districts of our cities to their old level—to set them on the platform even of a higher Christianity.

Can these people ever be raised? Can those "dry bones live?" "Where is the Lord God of Elijah?" are questions, distressing questions, which, when worn and weary, and disappointed, and cast down, and heartsick, we have been often tempted to ask. Of such times, we could say with David:—" We had fainted, unless we had believed to see the goodness of the Lord in the land of the living." But this voice of God came sounding down from Heaven, saying :—" Though ye have lain among the pots, yet ye shall be as the wings of a dove covered with silver, and her feathers with yellow gold." When ready to sink under a sense of our own feebleness, it said to us :—" The chariots of God are twenty thousand, even thousands of angels; the Lord is among them, as in Sinai, in the holy place." To the question, Can these lost ones be recovered? the answer came in these brave, and bold, and cheerful terms:—" I will bring again from Bashan; I will bring my people again from the depths of the sea, that thy foot may be dipped in the blood of thine enemies, and the tongue of thy dogs in the same." And, as he stood on the heights of inspiration, looking far away into distant time, and commanding an extent of prospect hid from common eyes, we heard the prophet announce the approaching of the promised event, a glorious gospel change:—" They have seen thy goings, O God; even the goings of my King in the sanctuary. The singers went before, the players on instruments followed after; among them were the damsels playing on timbrels. There is little Benjamin with the ruler, the princes of Judah with their council, the princes of Zebulon and the princes of Naphtali. Thy God hath commanded thy strength. Strengthen, O God, that which thou hast wrought for us. Sing unto God, ye kingdoms of the earth, O sing praises unto the Lord."

Yes. To put new vigor into his sinking energies, a man has only to "remember the years of the right hand of the Most High." How does the gospel of Jesus Christ, crowned with triumphs, point her sceptre not to families, nor hamlets, nor cities, but whole nations, raised from the lowest barbarism and the basest vices!

We cannot despair so long as we do not forget, that the power of God, and the wisdom of God, and the grace of God, have nothing to do within our shores which they have not done already. Are our lapsed classes rude and uncultivated, ignorant and vicious? So were our forefathers, when Christianity landed on this island. She took possession of it in Jesus' name, and conquered bold savages, whom the Romans could never subdue, by the mild yet mighty power of the gospel. God's "hand is not shortened that it cannot save, nor is his ear heavy that it cannot hear." Therefore, whatever length of time may be required to evangelize our city masses, however long we may be living before the period when a "nation shall be born in a day," whatever trials of patience we may have to endure, whatever tears we may have to shed over our cities, our tears are not such as Jesus wept, when he beheld Jerusalem.

No. Jerusalem was sealed to ruin—doomed beyond redemption. Our brethren, our cities are not so. We have not to mourn as those who have no hope. As on a summer day I have seen the sky at once so shine and shower, that every rain-drop was changed by sun-beams into a falling diamond, so hopes mingle here with fears, and the promises of the gospel shed sun-light on pious sorrows. Weep we may; weep we should—weep and work, weep and pray. But ever let our tears be such as Jesus shed beside the tomb of Lazarus, when, while weeping, groaning, he bade the bystanders roll away the stone—anticipating the moment when the grave at his command would give up its dead, and Lazarus be folded, a living brother, in the arms that, four days ago, had swathed his corpse. Be such our tears and anticipations. Sustained by them we shall work all the better; and all the sooner shall our heavenly Father embrace the most wretched of these wretched outcasts. Faith may be cast down, but cannot be destroyed. There is no reason, because we are "perplexed," ever to "despair." Black as the prospect looks, the cloud presents one aspect to the world, and another to the Christian. I stand on the side of it that lies next the sun. There, with the sun shining at my back and the black cloud in my eye, I see a radiant bow which spans its darkness, and reveals in heavenly colors mercy to a fallen world. "It is a faithful saying, and worthy of all acceptation, that Jesus Christ came into the world to save sinners." With the eye of faith fixed on that, we resume our work, and proceed still further to lay bare the state of the city—its sorrows for Christian balm, its sins for Christian cure.

We have turned your attention to the extent of intemperance, let us now

Secondly, *Attend to the effects of this vice.*

The Spartans, a brave, and, although heathens, in many respects a virtuous people, held intemperance in the deepest abhorrence. When Christian parents initiate their children in drinking habits, and—as we have seen and wondered at—teach them to carry their glass to infant lips, copy whom they may, the wise old Spartans are not their model. They were not more careful to train the youth of their country to athletic exercises, and from their boyhood and almost their mothers' breasts to "endure hardship as good soldiers" of Sparta, than to rear them up in habits of strictest, sternest temperance. It formed a regular branch of their national education. Why should it not of ours? It would be an incalculable blessing to the community. It would do incalculably more to promote domestic comfort, to guard the welfare of families, and secure the public good, than other branches that, while they go to improve the taste and polish the mind, put no real pith or power into the man. Well, once a year these Greeks assembled their slaves, and, having compelled them to drink to intoxication, they turned them out—all reeling, staggering, besotted, brutalized—into a great arena, that the youths who filled its benches might go home from this spectacle of degradation to shun the wine-cup, and cultivate the virtues of sobriety. Happy country! thrice happy land! where drunkenness was to be seen but once a year, and formed but an annual spectacle. Alas! we have no need to employ such unjustifiable means even for so good an end! We do not require to get up any annual show, from the pulpit to tell, or on the stage of a theatre to represent, its accursed, and direful, and disgusting effects. The lion is daily ravaging on our streets. He goes about "seeking whom he may devour."

Once a year, indeed, when church-courts meet, our city may present a spectacle which fools regard with indifference, but wise men with compassion and fear. A pale and haggard man, bearing the title of "Reverend," stands at the bar of his church. Not daring to look up, he bends there with his head buried in his hands, blushes on his face, his lips quivering, and a hell raging, burning within him, as he thinks of home, a broken-hearted wife, and the little ones so soon to leave that dear sweet home, to shelter their innocent heads where best, all beggared and disgraced, they may. "Ah, my brother" there! And ah, my brethren here, learn to "watch and pray, that ye enter not into temptation." See there the issue of all a mother's anxieties, and a father's self-denying and parsimonious toil, to educate their promising, studious boy. In this deep darkness has set for ever a brilliant college career. Alas! what an end to the solemn day of ordination, and the bright day of marriage, and all those Sabbaths when an affectionate people hung on his eloquent lips! Oh! if this sacred office, if the constant handling of things divine, if hours of study spent over the word of God, if frequent scenes of death, with their most awful and sobering solemnities, if the irremediable ruin into which degradation from the holy office plunges a man and his house along with him, if the unspeakable heinousness of this sin in one who held the post of a sentinel, and was charged with the care of souls—if these do not fortify and fence us against excess, then, in the name of God, "let him that thinketh he standeth, take heed lest he fall." You are confident in your strength, so was he. You can use without abusing, so once could he. I tell you I have seen ministers of the gospel charged by fame, dragged to the bar of their church, and degraded before the world as drunkards, whom once I would have as little expected to fall as I expect some of you—as you believe it possible that this vice shall yet degrade me from the pulpit, and cause my children to blush at mention of their father's name. Such cases are trumpet-tongued. Their voice sounds the loudest warning. In such a fall we hear the crash of a stately tree. Leave an ungodly world—deaf, stone-deaf to the voice of Providence—to quaff their cups, and make the fall of ministers "the song of drunkards;" leave them to say that all religion is hypocrisy, and see, in such a case, but the dropping of a mask from falsehood's face. Let that which emboldens them in sin teach you to stand in awe. For it seems to me as if, disturbed in his grave by the shock of such an event, the old prophet, wrapped like Samuel in his mantle shroud, had left the dead to cry in the ears of all the living, who regard with indifference the fall of a minister, "Howl, fir-trees, for the cedar is fallen."

On leaving a church-court, where he has seen so strange and dreadful a spectacle as a man of cultivated mind, a man of literary habits, a man of honorable position, a man of sacred character, sacrifice all,—the cause of religion, the bread of his family, the interests of his children, the happiness of his wife, his character, his soul,—all, to this base indulgence, no man, after such a terrible proof of the might and mastery of this tyrant vice, will be astonished at anything he may encounter in our streets. Yet if the soul of Paul was "stirred within him,"—stirred to its deepest depths,—when he saw the idolatry of Athens,

I think that he who can walk from this neighboring castle to yonder palace, nor groan in spirit, must have a heart about as hard as the pavement that he walks on. The degradation of humanity, the ragged poverty, the squalid misery, the suffering childhood, the pining, dying infancy, oh, how do these obliterate all the romance of the scene, and make the most picturesque street in Christendom one of the most painful to travel. They call the street in Jerusalem, along which tradition says that a bleeding Saviour bore his cross, the *Via Dolorosa;* and I have thought that our own street was baptized in the sorrows of as mournful a name. With so many countenances that have misery stamped on them as plain as if it were burned in with a red-hot iron—hunger staring at us out of these hollow eyes—drink-palsied men, drink-blotched and bloated women—sad and sallow infants who pine away into slow death, with their weary heads lying so pitifully on the shoulders of some half de-humanized woman—this poor little child, who never smiles, without shoe or stocking on his ulcered feet, shivering, creeping, limping along with the bottle in his emaciated hand, to buy a parent drink with the few pence that, poor hungry creature, he would fain spend on a loaf of bread, but dare not—the whole scene is like the roll of the prophet, "written within and without, lamentations, mourning, and woe." How has it wrung our heart to see a poor ragged boy looking greedily in at a window on the food he has no one to give him, and dare not touch,—to watch him, as he alternately lifted his naked feet, lest they should freeze to the icy pavement. He starves in the midst of abundance. Neglected among a people who would take more pity on an ill-used horse or a dying dog, he is a castaway upon the land. Of the throngs that pass heedlessly by him to homes of comfort, intent on business or on pleasure, there is no one cares for him. Poor wretch! O if he knew a Bible which none has taught him, how might he plant himself before us, and bar our way to church or prayer-meeting, saying, as he fixed on us an imploring eye, "Pure religion and undefiled before God" is to feed me —is to clothe these naked limbs—is to fill up these hollow cheeks—is to pour the light of knowledge into this darkened soul—is to save me—is not to go to house of God or place of prayer, but first coming with me to our miserable home, " to visit the widow and fatherless in their affliction, and keep thy garments unspotted from the world."

You can test the truth of these statements. You have only to walk along the street to verify them. Yet bad as it looks, and bad as it is, the street reveals not half the evil. I know that some look with suspicion upon our statements. They doubt whether matters below are so bad as we report. They insinuate that surely we are exaggerating existing evils. Well, there is nothing more easy, although there might be many things more noble, than to lie beneath bright skies, and amid gay company, and on a flowery sward, and dismiss with an incredulous smile the claims of suffering humanity. It were more like a man and a Christian to throw yourself into the bucket, seize the chain, go down into the pit and put the matter to the proof. We invite you to do that which will rudely dissipate every doubt, and bring you up, a better and wiser man, to say with Sheba's Queen, "The half was not told me." Meanwhile, come along with me, while I again travel over some bygone scenes.

Look there! In that corpse you see the cold, dead body of one of the best and godliest mothers it was ever our privilege to know. She had a son. He was the stay of her widowhood—so kind, so affectionate, so loving. Some are taken away from the "evil to come;" laid in the lap of mother earth, safe beneath the grave's green sod, they hear not and heed not the storm that rages above. Such was not her happy fortune. She lived to see that son a disgrace, and all the promises of his youth blighted and gone. He was drawn into habits of intemperance. On her knees she pleaded with him. On her knees she prayed for him. How mysterious are the ways of Providence! She did not live to see him changed; and with such thorns in her pillow, such daggers, planted by such a hand, in her heart, she could not live. She sank under these griefs, and died of a broken heart. We told him so. With bitter, burning tears he owned it; charging himself with his mother's death —confessing himself a mother's murderer. Crushed with sorrow, and all alone, he went to see the body. Alone, beside that cold, dead, unreproaching mother, he knelt down and wept out his terrible remorse. After a while he rose. Unfortunately—how unfortunate that a spirit bottle should have been left there—his eye fell on the old tempter. You have seen the iron approach the magnet. Call it spell, call it fascination, call it anything bad, demoniacal, but as the iron is drawn to the magnet, or as a fluttering bird, fascinated by the burning eye and glittering skin of the serpent, walks into its envenomed, expanded jaws, so was he drawn to the bottle. Wondering at his delay, they entered the room; and now the bed holds two bodies

—a dead mother, and her dead-drunk son. What a sight! what a humbling, horrible spectacle! And what a change from those happy times, when night drew her peaceful curtains around the same son and mother—he, a sweet babe, sleeping, angel-like, within her loving arms! "How is the gold become dim, the most fine gold changed!"

Or look there. The bed beside which you have at other visits conversed and prayed with one who, in the very bloom and flower of youth, was withering away under a slow decline—is empty. The living need it; and so its long, and spent, and weary tenant lies now, stretched out in death, on the top of two rude chests beside the window. And as you stand by the body—contemplating it—in that pallid face lighted up by a passing sun-gleam you see, along with lingering traces of no common beauty, the calmness and peace which were her latter end. But in this hot, sultry, summer weather, why lies she there uncoffined? Drink has left us to do that last office for the dead. Her father—how unworthy the name of father—when his daughter pled with him for his soul, pled with him for her mother, pled with him for her little sister, had stood by her dying pillow to damn her—fiercely damning her to her face. He has left his poor, dead child to the care of others. With the wages he retains for drink, he refuses to buy that lifeless form a coffin and a grave!

Or look there. You have found a young man, the victim of an incurable malady, sinking into the tomb. Dying is hard enough work amid all the comforts which wealth, and kindness, and piety can command; but in that winter time, with the frosty wind blowing through the broken panes, he is shivering while he seeks in the Bible its precious comforts; and how much his body is emaciated is too plainly visible beneath that single threadbare coverlet. You could not have stood that; no more could we. And where, at our next visit, are the warm comforts charity had provided? They have gone for drink! Gone for drink! For such purpose, what incarnate demons have plucked the blankets from that wasted form—steeling their iron hearts against his cries, his struggles, his unavailing tears? Accursed vice! that can sink man beneath the brutes that perish. The barbarous deed was done by a father's hand! That father, instigated and aided by her who had suckled him on her breast, a breast twice withered—by worse than age, deformed and dried up!

Did I say sinks man beneath the brutes that perish? It is a libel on creation to speak of a drunkard as a brute. The bear, when she refuses to desert her cub, when she makes the most daring, desperate efforts to protect her offspring, when, rearing herself on her hind feet, she stands up growling to face the hunter, and offer her shaggy bosom to his spear, extorts our admiration; as does the little creature which, when the spear is buried in a mother's heart, leaps on her dead body, and, giving battle to the dogs, attempts bravely, though vainly to defend it. Look at this case, and that. How beautiful is nature, how base is sin! Dr. Kane tells a story of a savage man in those arctic regions, where God has poured such affection into the bosom of the fiercest animals, which excites our pity. Noluk, when all other families in the time of famine had fled from their sick, remained faithful to his wife. She was dying. From waging fierce battle with the monsters of the deep, scaling the slippery iceberg, leaping the cracks of the ice-floe, homeward over the snowy wastes he drove his sledge each night, with food for her. The evening of his last visit arrives. He approaches the rude stone-hut, looks in, and through a window sees his wife a corpse, and his infant son sucking at her frozen breast. Instinct moved him to enter, pluck away the child, and make a daring effort to save its life and his own. But the burden of a sucking babe, the pressing fears of famine, these mastered parental affection; and, claiming our pity for the grief that stood in his eye and wrung his heart, he turned his dogs southward, nor crossed the threshold.

But what emotions do the cases I have told

you of awaken? To be matched by many and surpassed by some that I could tell—samples of the stock, what passion can they, what passion ought they to move, but the deepest indignation? Nor would I, however fiercely it may run, seek to stem the flood. The deeper it flows, the higher it rises, the stronger it swells and rolls, so much the better. I would not seek to stem, but to direct it—directing it not against the victims, but against the vice.

I pray you do not hate the drunkard; he hates himself. Do not despise him; oh, he cannot sink so low in your opinion as he is sunk in his own. Your hatred and contempt may rivet, but will never rend his chains. Lend a kind hand to pluck him from the mire. With a strong hand shatter that bowl—remove the temptations which, while he hates, he cannot resist. Hate, abhor, tremble at his sin. And for pity's sake, for God's sake, for Christ's sake, for humanity's sake, rouse yourselves to the question, What can be done? Without heeding others—whether they follow or whether they stay—rushing down to the beach, throw yourself into the boat, push away, and bend on the oar, like a man, to the wreck. Say, I will not stand by and see my fellow-creatures perish. They are perishing. To save them I will do anything. What luxury will I not give up? What indulgence will I not abstain from? What customs, what shackles of old habits will I not break, that these hands may be freer to pluck the drowning from the deep? God my help, his word my law, the love of his Son my ruling motive, I shall never balance a poor personal indulgence against the good of my country and the welfare of mankind. Brethren, such resolutions, such high, and holy, and sustained, and self-denying efforts, the height of this evil demands.

Before God and man, before the church and the world, I impeach Intemperance. I charge it with the murder of innumerable souls. In this country, blessed with freedom and plenty, the word of God and the liberties of true religion, I charge it as the cause—whatever be their source elsewhere—of almost all the poverty, and almost all the crime, and almost all the misery, and almost all the ignorance, and almost all the irreligion, that disgrace and afflict the land. "I am not mad, most noble Festus. I speak the words of truth and soberness." I do in my conscience believe that these intoxicating stimulants have sunk into perdition more men and women than found a grave in that deluge which swept over the highest hill-tops—engulphing a world, of which but eight were saved. As compared with other vices, it may be said of this, "Saul has slain his thousands, but David his tens of thousands."

3. *Consider what cure we should apply to this evil.*

The grand and only sovereign remedy for the evils of this world is the gospel of our Lord Jesus Christ. I believe that. There is no man more convinced of that than I am. But he rather hinders than helps the cause of religion who shuts his eyes to the fact, that, in curing souls, as in curing bodies, many things may be important as auxiliaries to the remedy, which cannot properly be considered as remedies. In the day of his resurrection Lazarus owed his life to Christ; but they that day did good service, who rolled away the stone. They were allies and auxiliaries. And to such in the battle which the gospel has to wage with this monster vice, allow me in closing this discourse to direct your attention. And I remark—

First, *That the legislature may render essential service in this cause.*

This is an alliance between church and state which no man could quarrel with. Happy for our country, if by such help, the state would thus fulfil to the church—the woman of prophecy—this apocalyptic vision:—" And the serpent cast out of his mouth, water as a flood, after the woman, that he might cause her to be carried away of the flood. And the earth helped the woman. And the earth opened her mouth, and swallowed up the flood which the dragon cast out of his mouth."

Many people feel no sympathy with the

sufferings of the lowest class. They are not hard-hearted; but engrossed with their own affairs, or, raised far above them in social position, they are ignorant of their temptations, and trials. Therefore they talk ignorantly about them; and seldom more so than when they repudiate all attempts of the legislature by restrictive Acts of Parliament to abate, if not abolish, this evil. They have their remedies. Some plead for better lodgings and sanitary measures; which we also regard as highly valuable. Some put their faith in education—an agent, the importance of which, to the rising generation, it is impossible to overestimate. Some seem to have no confidence in anything but the preaching of the gospel. To one or other of these, or the combined influence of them all, they trust for the cure of drunkenness—repudiating and deprecating all legislative interference. Now, I should like as much as they to see the very lowest of our people so elevated in their tastes, with minds so cultivated, and hearts so sanctified, that they could resist the temptations which on every hand beset them. But thousands, tens of thousands, are unable to do so. They must be helped with crutches till they have acquired the power to walk. They must be fenced round with every possible protection until they are "rooted and grounded in the love of God." In the country I have often seen a little child, with her sun-browned face and long golden locks, sweet as any flower she pressed beneath her naked foot, merry as any bird that sung from bush or brake, driving the cattle home; and with fearless hand controlling the sulky leader of the herd, as with armed forehead and colossal strength he quailed before that slight image of God. Some days ago, I saw a different sight—such a child, with hanging head, no music in his voice, nor blush but that of shame upon his cheek, leading home a drunken father along the public street. The man required to be led, guided, guarded. And into a condition hardly less helpless large masses of our people have sunk. I don't wonder that they drink.

Look at their unhappy and most trying circumstances. Many of them are born with a propensity to this vice. They suck it in with a mother's milk; for it is a well-ascertained fact that other things are hereditary besides cancer, and consumption, and insanity. The drunken parent transmits to his children a proneness to his fatal indulgence. The foul atmosphere which many of them breathe, the hard labor by which many of them earn their bread, produce a prostration which seeks in stimulants something to rally the system, nor will be debarred from their use by any prospect of danger, or experience of a corresponding reaction. With our improved tastes, our books, our recreations, our domestic comforts, we have no adequate idea of the temptations to which the poor are exposed, and from which it is the truest kindness to protect them. They are cold, and the glass is warmth. They are hungry, and drink is food. They are miserable, and there is laughter in the flowing cup. They are sunk in their own esteem, and the bowl or the bottle surrounds the drunkard with a bright-colored halo of self-respect, and, so long as the fumes are in his brain, he feels himself a man. "They drink to forget their poverty, and remember their misery no more."

Such indeed has been the only training, such are the physical, economical, moral, and religious conditions of large masses of the people, that their safety lies, not in resisting temptation, but escaping it. None know that better than themselves. How would thousands hail and bless the day, which, shutting up the drinking-shops, would preserve them from temptations which are their ruin, and to which they at length passively yield themselves; although, as one said, they know their doors to be the way to hell. Yet not passively, until this fatal pleasure has paralyzed the mind more even than the body. Many struggle hard to overcome this passion. There is a long and terrible fight between the man and the serpent that has him in his coils; between the love of wife and children and the love of drink. Never more manfully than some of them did swimmer struggle in his hour of agony — breasting the waves and straining every nerve to reach the distant shore. Would Parliament but leave this matter to these people themselves—would they for once delegate their powers of legislation to the inhabitants of our lowest districts—we are confident that, by their all but unanimous vote, every drinking-shop in their neighborhoods would be shut up. The birds, which are now drawn into the mouth of the serpent, would soar aloft on free and joyous wing to sing the praises of the hand that closed its jaws, of the heel that crushed its head. And so long as religion stands by—silent and unprotesting against the temptations with which men, greedy of gain, and Governments, greedy of revenue, surround the wretched victims of the basest vice—it appears to me an utter mockery for her to go with the word of God in her hand, teaching them to say, "Lead us not into temptation."

As a man, as well as minister of that blessed gospel which recognizes no distinction between rich and poor, I protest against the wrongs of a class that are to the full as unfortunate as they are guilty. They deserve succor rather than censure. They are more to be pitied than punished. And, assuming the office of their advocate, I wish to know why the upper classes of society should enjoy from the legislature a protection denied to those who stand more in need of it? Gambling-houses were proved before Parliament to be ruining the youth of the aristocracy. Nobility complained. Coronets and broad acres were in danger. Parliament rose to the rescue. She put forth her strong hand, and by a sweeping, summary, most righteous measure, put the evil down. It was also proved in Parliament that Betting-houses were corrupting the morals of our merchants' clerks, our shopmen, our tradesmen, and others of the middle classes of society. Once more Parliament rose up in its might, threw its broad shield over wealth and commerce, and closed every betting-house in the metropolis. Who talked then about the freedom of trade? When the honor of noble families, or the wealth of our merchants, and the honesty of their servants demanded protection, who talked about the liberty of the subject? Who proposed to leave these evils to be met by education and such means as education? I don't complain of, but commend the measures which Parliament adopted. Only, I want to know, if the virtues of humble families and the happiness of the poor are less worthy of protection than the wealth of bankers, and the honors of an ancient nobility? I want to know if the bodies of the higher and wealthier classes are of better clay, or their souls of finer elements, than those of the very lowest of the people? Yet I would undertake to prove that, year by year, thousands and tens of thousands of our poor lose character, virtue, fortune, body and soul, in those drinking-shops that glare upon the public eye—which the law does not forbid, but license. For every one the gambling or betting-house ruined, they ruin hundreds. I wish that those who govern this noble country should be able to say with Him who governs the universe, "Are not my ways equal?" Nor let our legislators be scared from their duty in this case, any more than they were in the other, by the allegation that to shut up the drinking-shop will not cure but rather aggravate the evil, by leading to illicit traffic and secret drinking. The removal of the temptation may not always cure the drunkard. But it will certainly check the growth of his class, and prevent many others from learning his habits—until sanguine men might entertain the blessed hope that, like the monsters of a former epoch, which now lie entombed in the rocks, drunkards may be numbered among the extinct races, classified with the winged serpents and gigantic sloths that were once inhabitants of our globe.

The subject before us is eminently calculated to illustrate the profound remark of one, who was well acquainted with the temptations and circumstances of the poor. He said:—"It is justice, not charity, that the poor most need." And all we ask is, that you be as kind to them as to the rich; that you guard the one class as carefully as you guard the other from the temptations peculiar to their lot. I am sorry to say—but truth and the interests of those who, however sunk and degraded, are bone of our bone and flesh of our flesh, require that I should say—that this is not done. The "poor," says Amos, "are sold for a pair of shoes," and with us they are sold to save the wealth of the rich. In this I make no charge which I am not prepared to prove. For example:— Certain measures were proposed in Parliament with the view of promoting the comforts and improving the moral habits of the common people. It was admitted that these, by introducing weak French and Rhenish wines in room of ardent spirits and strongly intoxicating liquors, would be attended with the most happy and desirable result. Yet they were rejected. And rejected because their adoption, although it saved the people, would damage the revenue. As if there was not money enough in the pockets of the wealthy, through means of other taxes, to meet the debts of the nation and sustain the honor of the Crown. How different the tone of morals even in China! The ministers of that country proved to their sovereign that he would avert all danger of war with Britain, and also add immensely to his revenue, if he would consent to legalize the trade in opium. He refused, firmly refused, nobly refused. And it were a glorious day for Britain, a happy day for ten thousand miserable homes—a day for bonfires, and jubilant cannon, and merry bells, and bannered processions, and holy thanksgivings, which saw our beloved Queen rise from her throne, and in the name of this great nation address to her Lords and Commons the memorable speech of that pagan monarch:—"I will never consent to raise my revenue out of the ruin and vices of my people." With such a spirit may God imbue our land!—"Even so come, Lord Jesus. Come quickly."

Secondly, *That the example of abstaining from all intoxicating liquors would greatly aid in the cure of this evil.*

No principle is more clearly inculcated in the word of God, and none, carried out into action, makes a man more Christ-like than self-denial. "If meat make my brother to offend, I will eat no flesh while the world standeth, lest I make my brother to offend." That is the principle of temperance, as I hold it. I cannot agree with those who, in their anxiety for good, attempt to prove too much, and condemn as positively sinful the moderate use of stimulants. But still less sympathy have I with those who dare to call in Jesus Christ to lend his holy countenance to their luxurious boards. It is shocking to hear men attempt to prove, by the word of God, that it is a duty to drink—to fill the wine-cup and drain off the glass.

I was able to use without abusing. But seeing to what monstrous abuse the thing had grown, seeing in what a multitude of cases the use was followed by the abuse, and seeing how the example of the upper classes, the practices of ministers, and the habits of church members were used to shield and sanction indulgences so often carried to excess, I saw the case to be one for the apostle's warning:—" Take heed lest by any means this liberty of yours become a stumbling block to them that are weak." Paul says of meat offered unto an idol:—"Meat commendeth us not to God; for neither if we eat are we the better, neither if we eat not are we the worse." And will any man deny, that, save in medical cases, I can with the most perfect truth adopt the words of inspiration, and say of these stimulants what Paul says of meat:—"Drink commendeth us not to God; for neither if we drink are we the better, and neither if we drink not are we the worse." On the contrary, the testimony of physicians, the experience of those who, in arctic cold or Indian heat, have been exposed to influences the most trying to the constitution; the experience also of every one who has exchanged temperate indulgence for rigid abstinence, have demonstrated that, if we drink not, we are the better. There is no greater delusion in this world than that health, or strength, or joyousness is dependent on the use of stimulants. So far as happiness is concerned, we can afford to leave such means to those who inhabit the doleful dens of sin. They cannot want them. They have to relieve the darkness with lurid gleams. They have to drown remorse in the bowl's oblivion. They have to bury the recollection of what they were, the sense of what they are, and the foreboding of what they shall be—as one of them said, "we poor girls could not lead the life we do without the drink."

Grant that there were a sacrifice in abstaining, what Christian man would hesitate to make it, if by doing so he can honor God and bless mankind? If by a life-long abstinence from all the pleasures which the wine-cup yields I can save one child from a life of misery, I can save one mother from premature grey hairs, and griefs that bring her to the grave, I can save one woman from ruin, bringing him to Jesus I can save one man from perdition, I should hold myself well repaid. Living thus, living not for myself, when death summons me to my account, and the Judge says, Man, where is thy brother? I shall be found walking, although at a humble distance, in the footprints of him who took his way to Calvary. He said, "If any man will come after me, let him deny himself, and take up his cross daily, and follow me." This cross, which has been held high in the battlefield by men nobly fighting for their faith, which rose above the scaffold red with martyr's blood, which has been borne by missionaries to pagan lands, may be carried into our scenes of social enjoyment, and, a brighter ornament than any jewels flashing on beauty's breast, may adorn the festive table. If this abstinence is a cross, all the more honor to the men who carry it. It is a right noble thing to live for God and the good of men.

I attempt to dictate on this subject to no man. Believing it to be one specially open to the apostolic rule, "Let every man be fully persuaded in his own mind;" I would yet venture to appeal to my brethren in the ministry, and to the members of every Christian church. There cannot be a doubt, not the shadow of a doubt, that if, devoting yourselves Christ-like to the glory of God and the good of men, you saw it to be your duty to embrace the principle of abstinence, the result would be remarkable. Such would be the influence of your example within your own household, and outside in your different neighborhoods, and such also the power which you could exercise in the Parliament of our country, that intemperance with all its direful damning consequences would be, to a great extent and in time, banished from the land. What a land ours then would be! Relieved from this mill-stone which hangs about her neck, and weighs her down and bends her giant power to the earth, into what an attitude and height of power would she rise? Who then would dare to insult her flag? Who then would dare to cross her path, when she went forth in her might and virtue to assert the liberties of the world—to break the fetters of the slave or fight the battle of the oppressed. She would hear no more taunts from the slave-holders of the West or the despots of the South. Her piety, and sobriety, and virtues, preserving salt, elements of national immortality, she might hope to be exempted from the fate of all preceding empires, that, one after another, in unfailing succession, have gone down into the tomb.

This moral revolution in our national habits, this greatest of all reforms, every one can engage in. Women and children, as well as men, can help it onwards to the goal. It is attainable, if we would only attempt it. It is hopeful, if we would but give the subject a fair consideration. Why should not the power of Christianity, by its mighty arguments of love and self-denial, lead to the disuse of intoxicating stimulants, and so achieve that which Mahommedanism and Hindooism have done? Must the cross pale before the crescent? Must the divine religion of Jesus, with that God-man upon the tree for its invincible ensign, blush before such rivals, and own itself unable to accomplish what false faiths have done? Tell us not that it cannot be done. It can be done. It has been done—done by the enemies of the cross of Christ—done by the followers of an impostor—done by worshippers of stocks and stones. "And their rock is not like our

Rock." If that is true—and it cannot be gainsaid—I may surely claim from every man who has faith in God, and loves Jesus, and is willing to live for the benefit of mankind, a candid, a full, and a prayerful consideration of this subject. But, whatever be the means, whatever the weapons you will judge it best to employ, when trumpets are blowing in Zion, and the alarm is sounding and echoing in God's holy mountain, come—come to the help of the Lord against the mighty, crowd to the standard, throw yourself into the thick of battle, and die in harness fighting for the cause of Jesus. So "to live is Christ, and to die is gain."

SERMON IV.

"When he beheld the city, he wept over it."—LUKE xix. 41.

A REMARKABLE incident occurred during the last unhappy, and—since it was waged between brethren, sprung of a common parentage, and holding a common faith—I will add, unnatural war between our country and America. We had taken a prize. A very gallant young officer was placed in command of her. Unfortunately for us, as the event proved, her original captain and part of his crew, were not transferred to another ship, but allowed to remain on board. The British lieutenant had a number of our own brave men sent along with him—a force sufficient to work the ship, and, in a fair stand up fight, to overpower the prisoners, should they attempt to retake the vessel. Hoisting British colors, they parted company with the capturing ship, and with our officer on the quarter-deck made homeward with their prize. Onward the ship ploughs her way through the billows, and all seems safe. After some time, the American captain accosts our officer on the deck. He desires him to give up his sword and the command of the vessel. Surprised, indignant at such a strange and insolent demand, he prepares to resist. Whereupon the American, drawing a pistol from his belt to meet the other's sword, conscious of his power, but unwilling to shed the blood of a gallant man, coolly added:—"You must surrender, your men are all drunk below." The officer, however, did resist, and was shot dead. His life was thrown away; his gallant bravery was of no avail. Intemperance had betrayed the ship—the men had all been drenched with rum and laudanum.

This story is as instructive as tragic. For that ship, won not by fair fighting, but a foul trick, carrying at her mast head foreign colors, with a new commander on her quarter-deck, her crew below in irons, and her head brought round, and bearing away to the coasts of the enemy, presents to my eye a picture of the fate of many. By the same instrumentality they are seduced—betrayed into the hands of the Adversary. By intemperance, also, they are "taken captive of the devil at his will." Had there been no intoxicating liquors on board, had she sailed under the temperance flag, as it is called, that ship had not been lost, nor had her crew pined in foreign prison, nor had that gallant man, who had otherwise returned to his mother's arms, rich with prize money, and wearing laurels on his brow, lain there—a bleeding corpse upon the deck. There is no doubt of that. No man will attempt to deny that. And we appeal to your candor, if this is not as true, that thousands of our fellow-creatures had never been lost, many a poor servant girl had never forfeited her character and lost her place, many a tradesman had never lost his employment and been reduced to beggary, many a merchant had never lost his business and become a bankrupt, many a woman had never lost her virtue and wrecked her peace, many a man and woman had never lost both soul and body, if they had practised habits of abstinence. Drink has been their ruin. And their ruin had never been, if, so to speak, they had sailed the voyage of life with no intoxicating liquors on board. That *ruse de guerre* so successfully played on the "high seas," is one of Satan's most common, every-day services. These stimulants weaken the reason, while they inflame the passions. They quicken corruption, whilst they stupify conscience. And I believe —and who does not?—that but for the use of them, thousands would never have taken that first step in sin, which, step by step, and step by step, has conducted their feet down to ruin.

Convinced as I am—and, as I presume you are—of the innate depravity of human nature, I think that we have no need to increase the dangers of temptation and arm it with additional powers. They who carry gunpowder on board are careful of fires and lights—nor careless even of a spark, lest that, reaching the magazine, should blow the ship out of the water, and the crew into eternity. Believing as I do in the weakness of our nature, I think that we have little need by anything to increase our proneness to fall. The path of a man, even of a man on the highway to heaven, is never one of perfect safety, and is often one of imminent danger. It resembles those mountain-passes in the Higher Alps, where the narrow road, its broken surface, and the dizzy depths below, require a steady foot and the coolest head; one false, one stumbling step, and you are gone, over the rocks, sheer down a hundred fathoms, where the angry torrent foams in the bottom of a gloomy gorge, white as the snows it flows from; or—no happier fate—you are left lying, mid-way down, on some projecting crag, a mangled mass—a banquet for the vultures. Many such dangerous passes there are in the journey of life. The very next turn, for anything we know, may bring us on one. Turn that projecting point which hides the path before you, and you are suddenly in circumstances which demand that reason be strong, and conscience be tender, and hope be bright, and faith be vigorous, and the prayer be ready to spring from our lips, "Lord, hold up my goings, that my footsteps slip not."

I leave this part of my subject; but before I leave it, let me appeal to the love and anxieties of Christian parents—of every parent. If you believe, as a foolish mother once said to me, when gently warning her to guard her child, "There is no ill, sir, about my child," I have nothing now to say, but, God pity the child that has such a mother. Hoping better things of you, brethren, let me put it to you, whether you are not most likely to preserve your children from many temptations, and lay a good foundation for their well-doing, and your own parental comfort, by training them up in the early and entire disuse of what is the ruin of so many families, the curse of so many homes, and what, if not taught to like, they have no craving for. Apply to this, as to other things, the lesson of holy Scripture, "Train up a child in the way he should go, and when he is old, he will not depart from it." Surely, oh surely, we have no need, either for ourselves or children, to create temptations—rashly to court dangers which we can avoid. It is a hard fight at the best to get to heaven. We shall get fighting enough without challenging it. We should leave vaporing fools to repeat the bravado of the Philistine. Let no man step out from the ranks of the cross, even from the side of Christ, to bid defiance to the devil, saying, "Give me a man to fight with." Our safety lies most, not in fighting but in fleeing temptation—in ever remembering this solemn truth, "The righteous scarcely are saved."

These views I press on no man, but present to the candid and prayerful consideration of all. But if these views do not meet your favor, nor commend themselves to your conscience before God, if you think it best and wisest to leave yourselves and your children, and others, exposed to the terrible temptations which I think it Christian prudence to avoid, then there is the more need that you be fully armed for the battle. To save our country and our religion, there is the more need that you apply a prompt and effectual remedy to other two great evils, to which, as belonging to the sins and sorrows of the city, I now request your attention.

III. Ignorance, or want of education.

First, *Let us look at this evil as it exists among the lowest classes.*

Our blessed Lord was born in a stable. And the stable which marked the beginning, like the cross which stood at the end of his life, has been always regarded as a prominent feature of his humiliation. Yet I have seen some who were born in even more humiliating circumstances. Many years ago—for the subject is not new to us—we were attempting to sound the depths of city-sins and city-sorrows. When engaged in this pursuit, we visited the police-office at dead of night. It was a chamber of horrors. There, lost, guilty, degraded humanity was represented by a wretched object dying beside the fire, in the last stages of consumption—the sister of a minister of the gospel. She had led a life of the lowest infamy, and, a houseless outcast, was draining off there the dregs of a bitter cup. But if that and many other cases filled us with horror, some moved our pity; none more than two sleeping infants, the twin offspring of a poor wandering creature who had given birth to them the day before within the walls of that police-office. What a fate was theirs! What an ominous beginning! What a life of hardship, cruelty, sin, and misery lay before these two unconscious innocents! The shadow of their birth-place was thrown black and forward on their future destiny. It needed no seer to stand by that rude crib and tell their fortune. They had hardly a chance in life. They had heaven in death; and nowhere had death looked less grim than in that grim birth-chamber, had he come and plucked these two buds from the parent-tree, that they might blow in heaven on Jesus' breast.

These infants were types of a class, with which, although somewhat better born, yet in no way better bred, our large cities swarm.

People—people who find it difficult enough, with all the appliances of a good education and religious training, to keep their children in the paths of honesty and rectitude—wonder that there is so much crime. If they saw what some of us have seen, and knew what some of us have known, they would still wonder, but wonder there was so little crime. To expect from those who have been reared in the darkest ignorance, and in a very hot-bed of temptations, anything else but crime, is sheer folly. A man might as well wonder that he does not see wheat or barley growing in our streets—where plough never goes, and no seed is sown. What can a farmer expect to find in a field left fallow, abandoned to nature, to the floating thistle-down and every seed furnished with wings to fly, but evidence of his own neglect in a rank, vile crop of weeds?

Look at the case of a boy whom I saw lately. He was but twelve years of age, and had been seven times in jail. The term of his imprisonment was run out, and so he had doffed the prison garb and resumed his own. It was the depth of winter; and having neither shoes nor stockings, his red, naked feet were upon the frozen ground. Had you seen him shivering in his scanty dress—the misery pictured on an otherwise comely face—the tears that went dropping over his cheeks as the child told his pitiful story—you would have forgotten that he had been a thief, and only seen before you an unhappy creature more worthy of a kind word, a loving look, a helping hand, than the guardianship of a turnkey and the dreary solitude of a jail.

His mother was in the grave. His father had married another woman. They both were drunkards. Their den, which is in the High Street—I know the place—contained one bed, reserved for the father, his wife, and her child. No couch was kindly spread for this poor child, and his brother, a mother's son— then also immured in the jail. When they were fortunate enough to be allowed to lie at home, their only bed was the hard bare floor. I say fortunate enough, because on many a winter night their own father hounded them out. Ruffian that he was, he drove his infants weeping from the door, to break their young hearts and bewail their cruel lot in the corner of some filthy stair, and sleep away the cold dark hours as best they could—crouching together for warmth, like two houseless dogs. A friend listened with me to that cruel tale; and when he saw the woe, the utter woe in that child's face, the trembling of his lip, the great big tears that came rolling from his eyes, and fell on one's heart like red-hot drops of iron, no wonder that he declared, with indignation flashing in his eyes, "They have not a chance, sir, they have not a chance." In circumstances as hopeless, how many are here—in every large city of this kingdom!

Yonder castaway, who has seen the ship go down, with all her shrieking crew, and, floating away upon his raft, has been borne along by sea currents over a shoreless ocean, has got a chance. These weeds, that are swung by the waves and give verdure to the deep, these sea-shore birds, on which his lank and hungry dog stands ready to spring, indicate the neighborhood of land; and we almost seem to see it looming through the fog-bank, on which his eye, kindling with hope, and shaded by his hand from the glare of the sun, is fixed, as he bends forward with such intent and eager gaze!

But to the castaway of the land, however, "hope is none." None, unless God in heaven pity him, and fill our hearts with one wave from the ocean of his infinite love. By the depraved habits of their parents, by the dangerous associations of the street, by their cold and nakedness, their hunger and houselessness, and most of all, I think, by the very hostility bred within them against a community that has only added punishment to neglect, and "persecuted them whom God had smitten," they are impelled on evil. We do nothing to instruct them. We leave them exposed to temptations, before which the best of us would go down. Thus we first condemn them to crime, and then condemn them to punishment. And where is the justice of that? I have often felt, that had society meted out to me the measure which she had meted out to them, I would have hated her, and sought vengeance for my cruel wrongs—unless this nature had been changed and mellowed and tempered by the grace of God. Thanks be to God, the eyes of the nation—long, too long sealed—are now opening to its duty. We hail the dawn of a better day. The time is coming, God speed it on! when, as they read how thousands of children, whom we left to grow up in ignorance and sin, were thrown into jail, were punished for crimes which their parents trained and their circumstances forced them to—were shut up, mere boys and girls, for weary months of solitude, within the four walls of a cell which they left stamped with infamy, and doomed to ruin—a succeeding generation will read the story of our inhumanity and injustice with feelings of astonishment and indignation. There is gross injustice in all this. We visit the iniquity of the fathers upon the children. We punish the innocent and let the guilty go free. And our treatment of these poor suffering creatures is calculated to excite feelings in every just and generous mind, if not as intense, yet akin to the horror with which we read, how in the days of George II. they brought out two infants, a boy of twelve and a girl of eleven years old, and strung them up on the same gallows before the face of an amazed and angry heaven.

Meanwhile, there are thousands, and tens of thousands, and hundreds of thousands, of the children of this land, who are growing up strangers to the benefits and blessings of education. Ignorance is their sole inheritance. And in regard to them, I may put into the mouth of our country the very complaint which the prophet puts into the mouth of God, "My people are destroyed for lack of knowledge." They are punished for it, impoverished for it, imprisoned for it, banished for it, and hanged for it. The "voice heard in Ramah, lamentation and bitter weeping," falls upon our ear. Rachel is weeping for her children. Victims of parental cruelty, I call on humanity to bless them with the protection which she extends in this country to the lower animals. Subjects in time past only of punishment, I next call on justice to sheathe the sword, and lift up her shield, and throw it over the heads of these unhappy children. And next I call on religion to leave her temples, and, like a mother seeking a lost child, to go forth to the streets, and gather in these infants for Jesus' arms—save these gems for a Saviour's crown.

Second, *Let us look at this evil as it exists among the working classes.*

The want of education is not confined to the lowest of the people. Many of the children of our working classes begin the business of life before they have finished that of education, and not a few of them even before they have begun it. The condition of our labor market lies as a heavy curse upon the nation. It is an evil poorly compensated by the growth of wealth, and that more general diffusion of the comforts of life in which we otherwise heartily rejoice. Unfortunately, in fant labor is remunerating now-a-days in the way of work, as it used to be in the way of mendicancy. In consequence of this, God's providence and man's plans are in collision—in direct collision. Heaven and earth are at war. The roar of machinery deafens the ear of tender childhood. The boy grows pale upon the loom, and the girl grows stunted by the whirling wheels, who should be drinking in knowledge at its fountains, or rushing from school to play with the lambs upon the flowery sward, or chasing the butterfly by the laughing stream, or gathering health and strength, beauty and symmetry where the bee collects her honied stores, for working days and winter-time. The click of shuttles and deafening noise of the manufactory are in ears that should be filled with no sound but the shouts and laughter of play, the melody of singing birds, or the hum of the busy school.

The harmony of nature is disturbed, and the effects of that disturbance on the physical, moral, and religious condition of our people are lamentable—and threaten to be more so.

Children are able to support before they have sense to guide themselves. Before God has fitted or ever intended them to be so, they are independent of parental control. Hence domestic discord, hence household rebellion, hence the defiance of parental authority. Too early removed from school, hence the spread of ignorance. Thrown in their very childhood into the company of hoary sin, hence their morals are corrupted. They are initiated into the mysteries of vice before they have the power to practise it. Without a parent's hand to guide the reins, before reason and principle have had time to assume their legitimate authority, the passions get it all their own headlong way. And in the fate of a carriage which has none to drive, but strong wild horses to drag it on; or, in the fate of a bark which, having broken loose from her moorings, catches the gust in her wide-spread sail, ere helm is hung or helmsman stands by the wheel—in that inevitable crash, in that shattered wreck—are symbolized the fate of many. Born in our great centres of manufacture, sent to work when they should be sent to school or continued at it, and earning wages sufficient to maintain themselves before reason is developed and principles are confirmed, they laugh at parental control, and in seeking to be their own masters become the slaves of their own master passions.

This is neither time nor place to show the extent of this evil, unless to say that, while the most extraordinary errors may lurk under general statistics, the public judging by them alone, may cherish the delusion that all is right when much is wrong. The actual truth may be best arrived at by selecting some particular locality, and subjecting it to a close and searching examination. We have done so in the Pleasance—a district of the city where we are about to build a church, and where, through our missionary and his allies, we have labored for four years with such remarkable success. There are worse, far worse districts than that in this city. There are many much worse in every large city in the kingdom. Yet there, in an area containing two thousand of a population, we found, when we entered on our labors, no fewer than two hundred children growing up without education—who should have been at school, and were not. They were not without schools, yet with these in the neighborhood they were without schooling. They had teachers within reach of them yet they were not taught. Now this is a very instructive fact. The plain and very important inference to be deduced from that fact is this, that while it is the duty of the state to provide the means of education, it is no less her duty to see that they are used. In the United States of America—a country where, perhaps, more than in any other, the value of education is thoroughly understood —the means of educating all the people are amply and in many instances freely provided. Yet by one of their last reports, complaints appear to come from every part of the country, that many parents neglect to send their children to school. This evil has begun to grow in America, which in our own land has reached so gigantic a size. Years of experience and observation, which were spent among the lower and lowest classes of the people, have produced in my mind the rooted conviction that, although public or private benevolence may plant schools in our streets, thick as trees in the forest, the evil never will be cured. From many a dark locality the city will continue to cry, "My people are destroyed for lack of knowledge," unless the state insist on this, that every child who should be, shall be at school.

From a system of trade which offers up our children in sacrifice to the Moloch of money, and builds fortunes in many instances on the ruins of public morality and domestic happiness—from the cupidity of some parents, and the culpable negligence of others — helpless childhood implores our protection. We laugh at the Turk who builds hospitals for dogs, but leaves his fellow-creatures to die uncured and uncared for. And we forget that dogs and horses enjoy, by Act of Parliament, a protection from cruelty among ourselves, which is denied to those whose bodies and whose souls we leave savage parents to neglect and starve. I lay it down as a principle, which cannot be controverted, and which lies, indeed, at the very foundations of society, that no man shall be allowed to rear his family, a burden, and a nuisance, and a danger to the community. He has no more right to rear wild men and wild women, and let them loose among us, than to rear tigers and wolves and send them abroad on our streets. What four-footed animal is so dangerous to the community, as that animal which unites the uncultivated intellect of a man to the uncontrollable passions of a beast?

We have a right to insist that this shall not be. Some rights I may waive. I may waive my right to a fortune. I may waive my right to the honors and emoluments of my office. I may abandon my claim to a competent living from those to whom I minister, and turn tent-maker like the great apostle. But if I have a right to interfere for the good of others, to shield the oppressed, to save the perishing, to instruct the ignorant—by any act on my part to benefit and bless my country—that is a right which I have no right to waive. God requires me to claim it and carry it into effect. Religion thus lends her holy sanction to the state, when she insists on a universal education. She commands society to take these children under its protection, and see to it, that all of them are trained through means of the school to be of service to the state. The parent who does not educate his children, should be regarded as a man who is not using his liberty, but is guilty of licentiousness. When will men cease to confound the two, and cease by applying the name of liberty to that which outrages the rights and destroys the liberties of others, to remind us of the saying of the celebrated woman who, when they were carting her to the guillotine, as the tumbril passed a statue that had been erected to Liberty rose to exclaim:—"O Liberty, what crimes have been committed in thy name!"

To ally that sacred name to the culpable and cruel neglect of parents who neither do their duty to their children nor to the state, is to help the cause of despotism, and make the name of liberty "stink in the nostrils" of the people. Let our country apply a prompt remedy to this evil, and upon the land which, with judgment to distinguish between liberty and licentiousness, and humanity to espouse the cause of the wronged, spread her mother wings over the least of these little ones, we may expect the blessing of Him who folded infants in the arms that sustain the world, and said, "Suffer little children to come unto me, for of such is the kingdom of heaven."

IV. The extent of irreligion in our large cities.

Much irreligion may be found among religious professors. To use a common saying, all is not gold that glitters. And there needs no other evidence of the fact, that irreligion does exist among religious professors, than the cold, callous, heartless indifference with which many hear of the sins and look upon the sorrows of their fellow-creatures. They could not do so if they were baptized into the nature as well as the name of Jesus Christ. In some cases the loss of a cattle-beast will affect the farmer, the loss of a few pounds on some speculation will distress the merchant, the loss of her raven locks, and the rose upon her cheek, and the fading charms that won admiration, will grieve the woman, more than the loss of immortal souls. Alas, the best of us have cause to pray for a deeper baptism in the spirit of Him, who, beholding the city, wept over it! Blessed Jesus! blessed Saviour, and blessed pattern! how didst thou leave the delights of heaven and thy Father's bosom, on a mission of most generous mercy! Thy love grudged no labor! Thine eye refused no pity! Thy ear was never shut against the story of distress! Thy hand was always ready to relieve the sufferer! From thy cradle to thy grave, thy whole life was passed in daily acts of loftiest self-denial, and, with the blood trickling down thy brows, and the heavy cross on thy lacerated back, upon thy way to Calvary, to save the vilest wretches and the chief of sinners, how dost thou turn round on us to say, "If any man will come after me, let him deny himself, and take up his cross daily and follow me! For whosoever will save his life, shall lose it, and whosoever will lose his life for my sake shall find it. For what is a man profited if he shall gain the whole world and lose his own soul? or, what shall a man give in exchange for his soul? For the Son of man shall come in the glory of his Father, with his angels, and then he shall reward every man according to his works."

The best of us have come far short, no doubt, of thus following Christ. Defects are many and great—leaving us no hope of salvation, but in the mercy of the Father, and the merits of the Son. Nor do we deny that there is a numerous class who follow the banner of the cross, but are, so to speak, mere camp followers—never fighting in the front of battle, nor found, but on a day of parade, among the ranks of the fighting men. They are professors of religion, because it is reputable and respectable to be so; because it keeps quiet an otherwise uneasy conscience;

because it helps them on in the world. They hold some such place in the Christian, as was occupied in the Jewish host, by the mixed multitude which, although not of Israel, followed Israel out of Egypt. But if that be certain, no less certain is this, that while in some cases there is a profession of religion without its reality, there is in no case the reality of religion without its profession. There may be leaves and blossoms also on a tree which bears no fruit, but without leaves and blossoms there can be none. The tree which, in high mid-summer, when skies are warm, and birds are singing, and flowers are blooming, and woods are green, stands there a skeleton form with its naked branches, has no life in it. It must be a cumberer of the ground.

Now, bearing this in mind, what an appalling picture of irreligion do our large towns present! Many years ago it was alleged that in our own city, containing a population of more than one hundred and fifty thousand souls, there were not fewer than forty thousand who had sunk into practical heathenism. They kept no Sabbath, they entered no house of God; bells might have been mute, pulpits silent, and churches shut for them. So far as they cared, or were concerned, the cross, with its blessed burden, might never have stood on Calvary. Just think of us, sitting at ease in Zion, with forty thousand neighbors perishing at our door—but one here, and another there, caring for their souls! Those who alleged this, those who had gone below to sound the well, and came up to report how the water was rising, were treated as alarmists. The sky was clear, the sea was calm, the ship was but slowly sinking, and so—all fears laughed away—the merry music struck up again, and the dance went on upon the deck. But since that period, another party has stept in—one not suspected of fanaticism or a sectarian spirit. The Government instituted a census, and its results have established the ability, and vindicated the integrity of those who were the first to sound the alarm. It is now proved, that not here only, where between forty and fifty thousand go to no church—not in Glasgow only, where more than a hundred thousand go to no church—not in London only, where more than ten hundred thousand go to no church; but that in all our large towns there are to be found immense, formidable, and growing masses over whom religion has no hold—who have parted from their anchors, and broken loose from all religious profession. Nor is that all. The plague has extended from the towns to the country. Many rural districts, which, some years ago, were the homes of a devout and decent peasantry, are now filled with a mining or manufacturing population, who know no Sabbath, read no Bible, and care neither for God nor man.

But instead of roaming over either the whole town or country, look again at that district of this city which we have begun to cultivate. In what state did we find its people, so far as attendance on divine worship was concerned? Well, upon entering on our work in the Pleasance—certainly, as I have already said, not the worst district of the town—we found more than one-third of its two thousand inhabitants, more than six hundred of the whole two thousand people, passing on to the grave as careless of their souls as if they had none to care for—living without the profession of religion—living without God or hope in the world—living, to all practical intents and purposes, heathens in a Christian land.

We, like other congregations of our own church and of other churches which have labored in the same work, have had already fruit of our labors. Let all other congregations, to whatever denomination of Christians they may belong, engage in a similar enterprise. Let each select their own manageable field of Christian work. Let us thus embrace the whole city, and cover its nakedness—although like Joseph, it should be robed in a coat of many colors. Let our only rivalry be the holy one of who shall do most and succeed best in converting the wilderness into an Eden, and causing these deserts to blossom as the rose. Like those allies on Crimean fields who forgot their old quarrels, and buried the recollections of the past in oblivion, let us all sit down together before this great fortress. They coöperated for the common good. Rebuking our wretched jealousies, and presenting us with a heroic, I had almost said a holy example of generous sympathy and indomitable energy, in the teeth of frost, and famine, and pestilence, and war, they clung to the rocks of that stormy shore. With mutual understanding and arrangements, they threw up their batteries, they pressed on their lines, they manned the trenches, they rushed to the assault—mingling the shouts of different nations in the same gallant charge, and the blood of different races in the same battle-field. And if nations, once hostile, there fought and fell together, there bled and died together, why should not different churches come to as common and cordial an understanding. If we make a united, I believe, with God's blessing, we shall make an irresistible assault upon these four formidable strongholds of Sin and Satan.

Let what we have done on a small scale in our selected district be done on a large one. We have brought the uneducated within the doors of the school. We have built up a Christian congregation out of a mass of ruins. We have gathered into the house of God many who were as sheep without a shepherd. We have done this by a devoted missionary —aided by Christian men and women who threw their energies into the work, and spent no small portion of their time among the dwellings of the people in household visitations. Let that which we have done on a small scale be done on a large one, and the lowest population of our cities may yet be raised, and the worst districts evangelized. This were done if every Christian family would select but one lost family as the object of their care, saying, Be that our work. It were done, if every convert would seek to make conversions; done, if every man who had himself reached the rock, would stretch out his hand to pull others up. The work before us—the work of raising and christianizing our masses—would be found, I believe, to be perfectly practicable, were it attempted in a systematic way, and on some such plan as this. Let the ministers or representatives of the different denominations within the city —Episcopalian, Baptist, and Independent, United Presbyterian, Free Church, and Established Church—meet, and form themselves into a real working Evangelical Alliance. Agreeing to regard all old divisions of parishes with an ecclesiastical right over their inhabitants as now-a-days a nullity, and so far as these are preventing Christian co-operation, and the salvation of the people, as worse than a nullity, let them map out the dark and destitute districts of the city—assigning a district to each congregation. Let every congregation then go to work upon their own part of the field, and giving each some 500 souls to care for, you would thus cover "the nakedness of the land." You would everywhere bring life into close contact with death, and cover the whole as the prophet with his own body did the dead body of the child. Every church-going family would have to charge itself with the care of one single family, with seeing that the children of that careless, godless household were got to school, and its members were brought out on the Lord's day to the church of the district, or their own place of worship, with visiting them in their sickness, and helping them over their difficulties, and by all Christian kindness promoting both their temporal and eternal interests. In this way the work were not only practicable, but amid all its difficulties comparatively easy. It would prove a blessing to the families visiting as well as to the families visited. And I am confident that it would bring down the blessing of God on itself, and on our country—in a few years presenting a result which would astonish earth and gladden heaven.

I have no hope of accomplishing this object if the churches are to be laced up by their old rules, and people are to leave everything to ministers and missionaries. Why should not he that heareth, as well as he that preacheth, say, Come? Why should not they that are preached to, preach? Our Lord gave to the disciples. Yes; but they gave to the people. And why should not some who now, on Sabbath-days, enjoy two services in the house of God, content themselves with one, and at the time of the other go forth to give what they have got? The bread would multiply in their hands. People may tell me they are not learned—I reply, that to tell these poor sinners of Jesus, whether beneath the roof of a house or the open roof of heaven, needs no learning. They need nothing but the love of Christ, zeal for souls, and the use of their mother tongue. Possessed of no qualifications but these; endowed with the Spirit, and ordained of Heaven, see what the first Christians did! They conquered the world! See what the first Methodists did! They changed the face of England. See what the church in Hamburgh did! Twenty years ago, five Christian men met there in a cobbler's shop. They also, when they beheld the city, wept over it. They resolved to form themselves into a church—a missionary church, with Hamburgh and its environs for the field of their labors. What their particular creed was, to what denomination of Protestants they belonged, I am not careful to inquire. High above the regimental colors of that little band floated the royal banner of the Cross. They fought for the crown of Jesus. They toiled, they watched, they labored for the salvation of souls. One article of their creed, one term of their communion, was this: — That every member of that Christian church should be a working Christian. So, in the afternoons and evenings of the Lord's day, they went forth to work, to gather in the loiterers by the highways and the hedges. Every member they gained was more than an accession to their numbers—he was an accession to their power. And with what results were their labors attended? These should encourage all other congregations and churches " to go and do likewise." That handful of corn is now waving in the golden harvests of many fields. That acorn is now shot up into a mighty oak that nestles the birds of heaven and braves the tempest, and throws a broad shadow on the ground. The church which was at first constituted of these five men, who met in an obscure and humble shop, has, in the course of twenty years, been blessed of God to convert many thousand souls, and bring some fifty thousand people under the regular ministrations of the gospel.

See what the Lord has wrought! In that experiment and its sublime results, in the rich effusion of the Spirit on the labors of these humble men and women—every one working in their own sphere, but all at work—who does not hear the voice of Providence saying, as it mingles with the songs of rejoicing angels, "Go and do likewise." And should any one come to me with the news that such and such an office-bearer, or member of this congregation, was preaching in our streets, I would reply with Moses: A young man came running to say, "Eldad and Medad do prophesy in the camp," and Joshua, jealous for his master's honor, interposed, saying, "My lord Moses forbid them." How noble his answer!

"Enviest thou for me? Would God that all the Lord's people were prophets, and that the Lord did put his Spirit upon them!"

Were such moral agencies established over all our cities, and wrought with the energy of men who trust in God, and are fired with the love of souls, were the churches to do their part in the matter of religion, and the state to do her part in the matter of education, our country might stand till the day of doom. Then it would appear, that although Britain bears no eagle on her banner, yet with her foot upon the "Rock of ages," and her undazzled eye fixed on the Sun of Righteousness, in this respect she belongs to the eagle tribe, that she can moult her wings and renew her youth. "For what saith the Lord, Hast thou not known? hast thou not heard, that the everlasting God, the Lord, the Creator of the ends of the earth, fainteth not, neither is weary? There is no searching of His understanding; he giveth power to the faint, and to them that have no might, he increaseth strength. Even the youths shall faint and be weary, and the young men shall utterly fall; but they that wait upon the Lord shall renew their strength; they shall mount up with wings as eagles, they shall run and not be weary, they shall walk and not faint."

But if this is not to be done, and nothing effectual is to be done to meet the evils that afflict our country, what " shall be the end of these things?" Unless they are met, met in time, and before the constitution sinks and loses all power to rally, the end of them must be the ruin of our land! Our cities, especially our large cities, being in this, as they are in every other country, the great centres of influence, if they increase in ignorance, irreligion, and immorality during the next century as they have done in the past, those who fear the God of heaven and profess the faith of Jesus Christ will find themselves a weak minority. We are just now rapidly moving on to such a dangerous crisis. That is the rock toward which the vessel of the state is drifting. And when that happens, it needs no augur to tell "what shall be the end of these things."

Take as types of their class the two largest cities in England and Scotland. Look at London and Glasgow. He must be blind who sees nothing alarming in the moral aspect of these commercial capitals. There, ignorance and irreligion are washing away the soil from beneath the lowest courses of the social fabric. Let that continue—let this undermining process go on till a convulsion come, and no power on earth can keep the pyramid from toppling over—burying throne and altar, and all that stands above, in a common ruin. The upper classes of society should know—God grant that they may not learn the lesson when it is too late!—that whatever be the distance between them, no elevation separates their interests from the lowest people; that there is a God who reigneth upon earth; and that, by a decree of Providence, as sure as those that rule the courses of tide or time, those who neglect the interests of others shall themselves suffer in the end. When the body of the people go down, they shall not perish alone; in them down goes a mighty ship, creating in its descent a tremendous whirlpool to engulph the rank and wealth, the religion and liberties, of our land. We are most concerned for the great body of the people, because it is in their virtues and piety that the power and permanence of kingdoms lie. They form the mass of the social fabric; and, although it will stand the shock, or survive the decay which destroys its lofty and more ornamental parts, let it be destroyed, and these are buried in the ruins. When the mass of the people cease to be pervaded with morality and piety (look at France, for instance), by a law as sure as that which, under certain conditions, changes wine into vinegar, the sweetest into the sourest things, liberty passes into licentiousness—an intolerable evil, from which to be relieved men submit their necks to the yoke of despotism. There is no choice for nations but the fear of God or the terror of man—the power of the Bible or the point of the bayonet.

When men die, corruption commonly begins after death; but when nations die, it always begins before it. And as in that man's gangrened extremities and swollen feet, and slow circulation, I see the heralds of death approaching—in these godless masses, sunk in ignorance, lost to the profession of religion, and even to the decent habits of civilized society, I see the most alarming signs of a nation's danger—unless remedies are promptly applied, the unmistakeable forerunners of a nation's death. Unless early, active, adequate measures are employed to arrest the progress of our social maladies, there remains for this mighty empire no fate but the grave—that grave which has closed over all that have gone before it. Where are the Assyrian and Egyptian monarchies? Where is the Macedonian empire? Where the world-wide power of Rome? Egypt lies entombed amid the dust of her catacombs. Assyria is buried beneath the mounds of Nineveh. Rome lives only in the pages of history, survives but in the memory of her greatness and the majestic ruins of the "Eternal City." Shall our fate resemble theirs? Shall it go to prove that Providence has extended the same law of mortality to nations that lies on men? That they also should struggle through the dangers of a precarious infancy; grow up into the beauty, and burn with the ardor, of youth; arrive at the vigor of a perfect manhood; and then, slowly sinking, pass through the blindness and decay of old age, until they drop into the tomb?

Under God, it depends upon ourselves whether that shall or shall not be our fate. Matters are not so far gone but it may be averted. A great French general, who reached the battlefield at sun-down, found that the troops of his country had been worsted in the fight. Unskilful arrangements had neutralized Gallic bravery, and offered the enemy advantages they were not slow to seize. He accosted the unfortunate commander. Having rapidly learned how matters stood, he pulled out his watch, turned his eye on the sinking sun, and said, "There's time yet to gain the victory." He rallied the broken ranks. He placed himself at their head. And launching them, with the arm of a giant in war, upon the columns of the foe, he plucked the prize from their hands—won the day. There is time yet, also, to save our country. There is no time to lose. To her case perhaps may be applied the words, which we would leave as a solemn warning to every worldly, careless, Christless man, "Behold now is the accepted time; behold now is the day of salvation."

APPENDIX.

Yet in these different kingdoms, &c.—P. 56.

IN Paris, we saw two persons who were drunk, one a soldier, the other an *ouvrier;* we also saw one soldier drunk in Brussels, and these three were all we saw drunk during a seven weeks' tour spent in various of the kingdoms, and large as well as small towns, of the Continent. We never saw a woman drunk, either during these seven weeks passed last summer on the Continent, nor during five months we spent many years ago in Paris. In none of these Continental towns, save in the Jewish quarter in Frankfort on the Maine, did we see anything like the foulness which in their closes, courts, and alleys, disgrace our large cities, and is enough to degrade their inhabitants. Save in the Canton of the Valais, a very poor and Popish district of Switzerland, we saw no rags, nor any such foul wretchedness, as is found in the low districts of all our large towns. We saw poverty sometimes, but it was decent poverty; and the worst clad children had none of that air of misery and sadness, worn by hundreds at home, who are the unhappy offspring of debauched and brutal parents. Public amusements and social enjoyments of an innocent kind are too little encouraged among us; and here the upper classes of society stand separated by too wide a gulph from the great mass of the people. There peer and peasant, king and subject, rub shoulders with each other in the same public gardens, and the humbler classes behave well because they are treated well.

In the charges of the English Judges.—P. 58.

Judge Coleridge: "There is scarcely a crime comes before me that is not, directly or indirectly, caused by *strong drink.*"

Judge Gurney : "Every crime has its origin, more or less, *in drunkenness.*"

Judge Pattison: "If it were not for this *drinking*, you (the jury) and I would have nothing to do."

Judge Alderson : "*Drunkenness* is the *most fertile source of crime;* and if it could be removed, the assizes of the country would be rendered mere nullities."

Judge Wightman : "I find, in every calendar that comes before me, one unfailing source, directly or indirectly, of most of the crimes that are committed—*intemperance.*"

Judge Williams : "Experience has proved that *almost all crime* into which juries have had to inquire, may be traced, in one way or other, to the habit of *drunkenness.*"

There is a city in England, &c.—P. 58.

During the Session of 1852, Mr. Hume, M.P., moved for a return of the number of persons taken into custody for drunkenness and disorderly conduct in Great

APPENDIX. 171

Britain and Ireland each year, from 1841 to 1851. From these returns it was found, that while in Liverpool, with a population of 400,000, 18,522 persons, and in Glasgow, with a population of 360,000, 14,870 persons were taken into custody by the police for the above offence; Manchester, with a population of 316,000, presented only 787 cases. It must be borne in mind, that while in Scotland the instructions of the police are most stringent, in Manchester no notice is taken of drunkenness unless in case of assault or breach of the peace, and not always then. Convinced from their own experience that so great a discrepancy as these returns exhibit arose from these and other circumstances, rather than from a *real* prevalence of sobriety among the population of our city, the committee of the Manchester and Salford Temperance Society determined to submit the question of the drinking habits of the people, *at least so far as Sunday is concerned*, to a rigid investigation. They resolved to watch all the houses in which intoxicating drinks are usually sold, and to keep an exact record of the number of visits paid to each during a certain time. It would be impossible to enumerate each separate district; a few, therefore, must suffice:—

St. Michael's Ward.—Inhabited principally by the operative class; a great portion by thieves, beggars, and prostitutes. Angel Street, Dych Street, Charter Street, Ludgate Hill, and adjoining streets, at two o'clock, on Sunday, May 28th, were crowded with men, women, and children, in rags and filth, some drinking in the streets, others gambling; in fact this district can only be described as a very hell upon earth. Most of the men taking this ward had to be changed every half hour, or hour; some were driven off by mobs, and others stoned. Number of houses taken, 162; visits, 13,738 men, 7862 women, 2905 children; total, 24,505, being 43 more than an average of 151.

District bounded by Great Jackson Street, Stretford Road, and Chester Road.—Several fights were reported, at which no police appeared; also one house filled with pigeon flyers, who were flying their birds the whole afternoon and evening from the front of the house; another house filled with dog-fighters, with their dogs, during the evening. There were one dog-fight, and two fights among the men frequenting the house, at none of which any policemen interfered. Number of houses, 96; visits, 6331 men, 4116 women, 1219 children; total, 11,666, being an average of 127 to a house.

Deansgate and Chester Road, including a beer-house on Victoria Bridge.—Swan Inn: 996 men, 590 women, 146 children; total, 1732. No. 274: 777 men, 676 women, 65 children; total, 1518. Farmers' Arms: 591 men, 582 women, 28 children; total, 1281. Crown Inn: 671 men, 360 women, 69 children; total, 1100. The Parsonage Inn, in the Parsonage: 858 men, 81 women, 6 children; total, 945. The person watching this house went in at one o'clock, being half an hour after it was opened, and counted 80 persons sat drinking. Trafford Arms, Victoria Bridge, a singing room: 549 men, 151 women, 420 youths; total 1120; visitors consist principally of young people. Ten other houses, with from 400 to 800 each. Total number of houses in Deansgate and Chester Road, 58; visited by 12,387 men, 6342 women, 1314 children; total, 19,845, being an average of $347\frac{3}{4}$ to a house.

APPENDIX.

The following is a general summary. It will be seen that while the proceedings of the committee extended over ten Sundays, yet, as no house was taken twice, a fair average of the attendance at each has been arrived at. The Committee are aware of no particular cause which could operate to render the results of one Sunday's census different from another; and it would have rendered observation much more difficult had not due caution and secresy been observed. The committee have every reason to believe in the perfect accuracy of the figures.

GENERAL SUMMARY OF VISITS DURING LEGAL HOURS.

Date.	Houses.				Men.	Women	Child'n.	Total.	
April 2	2				936	278	429	1,643	
" 9	8				2,163	902	51	3,116	
" 16	36				9,789	5,277	851	15,917	
" 23	57				7,056	3,981	692	11,729	
" 30	95				7,078	6,378	935	14,391	
May 7	100				6,699	4,088	1,109	11,896	
" 14	234				18,239	9,566	2,559	30,364	
" 21	329				27,684	16,322	6,201	50,207	
" 28	354				25,602	16,299	6,528	48,429	
June 4	222				14,878	8,518	4,230	27,626	
Total.	1,437				120,124	71,609	23,585	215,318	
		Vaults.	Public house.	Beer-house.	Total.				Aver'ge
		114	...	...	114	29,568	17,926	4,147	51,641	453
		...	127	...	127	14,880	7,947	2,835	25,662	202
		...	...	746	746	51,474	27,512	11,544	90,580	121
Mixed.		37	132	231	440	24,202	17,726	5,059	47,485	106¼
Total.		151	259	1,027	1,437	120,124	71,609	23,585	215,318	149¾

Including 54 policemen ON DUTY, who remained from five minutes to half an hour. Twenty public houses were found closed.

In closing this brief report of their labors, the committee beg to express their thanks to the various superintendents and teachers of Sunday-schools, and also to the several members of branch committees, who assisted in taking these statistics. The committee would earnestly direct the attention of every philanthropist to the fearful state of demoralization thus laid open; they would especially draw attention to the vast number of beer-houses in the city, 1572; to the class of persons keeping, as to those who visit, these *Dens.* It is a fearful fact that many of them are attended, and mainly supported, by mere youths of from 14 to 17 years of age.

With agencies for evil so potent and subtle—with temptations so numerous and so widely spread—and, above all, with a traffic in debauchery and crime protected and encouraged by *law*—what hope for the triumph of pure religion and virtue among our debased and sensual population? Does not the sin of Britain cry aloud for judgment? How long will Christians and philanthropists hesitate? How long shall paltry custom shield from infamy and disgrace those who profit by this sin? Let one earnest, heartfelt cry be sent forth, which, heard amid the echo of political and party strife, shall tell our legislators that the people of England will no longer groan under this oppressive burden of death; that they will labor and pray until the accursed traffic be swept from their midst forever!

Cause to thank God for that Act of Parliament.—.
P. 66.

Acts of Parliament cannot make men sober, otherwise than by removing the temptations which foster habits of intemperance. Forbes Mackenzie's Act, which

APPENDIX. 175

no one can wonder at those attacking who make their fortunes out of the vices of the people, has been attacked by others of whom better things might have been expected. The satisfactory accounts of its working which came from all parts of the country, should long ago have silenced its opponents; but they contrived, with a courage worthy of a better cause, to fight "upon their stumps," and continued to insist that this has proved a complete failure. It will rejoice every true friend of the people, and right-hearted Christian man, to find by the following report of Mr. Linton how completely that Act has succeeded.

The beneficial effects of it are very distinctly brought out in the following table. By that Act, which came into operation in 1854, no intoxicating liquors can be sold for consumption on the premises, save to "*bona fide*" travellers, before eight o'clock in the morning, and not at all between eleven o'clock on Saturday night and eight o'clock on Monday morning. This Act, which shuts up all drinking shops on the Lord's day, and also all inns, save to "*bona fide*" travellers, unfortunately applies only to Scotland.

NUMBER ON SUNDAYS.

	MALES.			FEMALES.			BOTH SEXES.		
	Found Drunk and kept till Sober.	Drunk when Apprehended.	Total.	Found Drunk and kept till Sober.	Drunk when Apprehended.	Total.	Found Drunk and kept till Sober.	Drunk when Apprehended.	Total.
1852	491	363	854	238	260	498	729	623	1,352
1853	427	384	811	214	280	494	641	664	1,305
1854	283	260	543	172	163	335	455	423	878
1855	234	194	428	155	185	340	389	379	768
1856	275	165	440	161	168	329	436	333	769

It has been alleged by the opponents of this Act (for, strange to say, it has had opponents), that the forced sobriety of the Sabbath-day only led to a greater excess in drinking on the Saturday or Monday. The unfounded nature of that statement is demonstrated by the following table:—

NUMBER ON SATURDAYS, SUNDAYS, AND MONDAYS.

	1852.	1853.	1854.	1855.	1856.
Saturdays....	1938	1879	1853	1783	1744
Sundays......	1352	1305	878	768	769
Mondays.....	1169	1236	1164	1038	852
Total......	4454	4420	3895	3589	3365

It has been alleged that not less than sixty millions of money.—P. 74.

That this statement is not an exaggeration, and that it is not in fact 30, but the enormous sum of 60 millions sterling, is spent year by year in Great Britain and Ireland on intoxicating liquors, is proved by the following statistics. They are extracted from the Journal of the Statistical Society of London, which originally appeared in a paper read by G. R. Porter, Esq., F.R.S., before the British Association.

The quantity of spirits of home production:

Paid by the consumers for British and Irish spirits consumed within the kingdom in 1849,	£17,381,643
Rum, ditto,.................................	3,428,565
Brandy, ditto,................................	3,281,250
Beer of all kinds, exclusive of that brewed in private families,.........................	25,383,165
	£49,474,623

APPENDIX. 177

Add to this sum the value of all the beer brewed in private houses, and also the money paid by the consumers for 5,582,385 gallons of foreign wine used in the United Kingdom, and there can be no doubt that at least 60 millions of money are annually spent by the people on what is, at the best a luxury, in most cases a pernicious, in all cases a dangerous, and in many cases a fatal indulgence.

It has been stated that 60,000 *lives are annually lost.*—P. 76.

In connection with this, I may state that the number of infant lives destroyed, through the neglect and starvation which they suffer in consequence of the drunken habits of their parents, it is impossible to calculate, but it must be frightful and enormous. Nothing struck us more, when we were accustomed to visit the families of the wretched classes, than to find how large a proportion of the children were cut off in early age; nor, when we saw the misery and crime which life would have had in store for them, could we regret to learn that they were safe in the churchyard.

The destruction of human life, directly caused by drunkenness, is the subject of a paper by F. G. P. Neison, Esq., F.L.S., a distinguished actuary, read before the Statistical Society of Sweden.

He shows that between the ages of 21 and 30 years, the mortality among drunkards is upwards of five times that of the general community. He states that if there be anything in the usages of society calculated to destroy life, the most powerful is certainly the inordinate use of strong drink. He produces tables which prove that the mortality among this class is frightfully high, and unequalled by the result of any other series of observations made in any class of the population of this country; and adds—"Sanitary agitators have frequently excited alarm about the wholesale havoc in human life going on in the badly-conditioned districts of some of our large cities; but no collection of facts ever brought under attention has shown so appalling a waste of life as exhibited in the above results."

Referring to tables founded on a broad basis, and wrought out with the nicest accuracy, he states:—"It will thus be seen, that an intemperate person, of age 20, has an equal chance of living fifteen years, while a person of the general population of the country, at the same age, has an equal chance of living 44 years longer. Again, at age 30, the intemperate person has an equal chance of living 13 years, and the other 36 years. Also, at age 40, the chance of the one is 11 years, and of the other 28 years."

The effect of intemperance upon different classes of the people, as given in his tables, is full of warning, and curious, although such as we might expect. The average duration of life, after the commencement of intemperate habits, is—

Among mechanics, laborers, and working men, . . . 18 years.
" traders, dealers, and merchants, ... 17 "
" professional men, and gentlemen, ... 15 "
" females, ... 14 "

Let all the kingdom listen to the weighty words of its Prime Minister. Lord Palmerston, in addressing the laborers, at the annual meeting of the Laborers' Encouragement Society, said :—" It is the duty of all parents to see that their children are well and properly educated —that they are early instructed, not merely in book learning, in reading and writing, and acquirements of that kind, but instructed in the precepts which indicate the difference between right and wrong, and that they are taught the principles of religion, and their duty towards God and man. Now, the way in which that can be done, is by the father and mother building up their household upon that which is the foundation of all excellence in social life—I mean a happy home (applause). Now, no home can be happy if the husband be not a kind and affectionate husband, and a good father to his children. Bearing this in mind, he must avoid two great rocks on which too many men in the humbler ranks make shipwreck—the tobacco shop and the beer shop. The first ruins his health, and leads to all kinds of disease. If he were a man living on a desert island, and isolated from society, this might be a matter of comparatively little importance, and he might ruin his constitution just as he pleased; but the laboring classes must remember that their health and strength are the support of their families, and if they ruin the one, and recklessly waste the other, they not only injure themselves, but do irreparable damage to those who are depending upon them. So much for the use of tobacco, which many, to their detriment, indulge in. But the beer shop and public house go further, because the habits there contracted not only lead to the degradation of the individual and the impoverishment of his family, but they lead to offences and crimes which tend to place the man in the condition of a felon and a convict. No man who indulges in drink can fail to feel degraded when he recovers from his intoxication, and that sense of degradation leads him again to drown his cares in renewed intoxication, and from step to step he falls into the lowest condition that human nature can be degraded to."

I charge it with the murder of innumerable souls.—
P. 105.

Many illustrations of this charge suggest themselves. Let us select, for example, the case of Sabbath school scholars. Look at the fatal influence which drink has been found to exert in those connected with Sabbath schools, and to what a lamentable and frightful extent it has neutralized all their blessed influences. In a letter which Mr. Logan addressed to the editor of the *British Banner*, he states:—" I have been in the habit of visiting prisons, and conversing with criminals almost weekly, for upwards of twelve years. My observations extend to almost every large prison in the United Kingdom. For the last eight years I have been trying to ascertain what proportion of our prison population have been connected with Sunday schools. When collecting information from prisoners, it has ever been a general rule with me to prevent them, as much as possible, from becoming acquainted with the main object of the visit. I record a few facts which refer to different parts of the country. I visited 78 of the 88 prisoners who were tried at the Glasgow assizes, in September, 1848. Seven of these could neither read nor write: of the remaining 71 not less than 38 males and 24 females—total, 62—had been connected with Sabbath schools. A number of both sexes had been in attendance at Sunday schools for three, four, five, six, seven, nine, and even ten years. To prevent anything like deception on this point, I cross-questioned them as to the locality of the schools, the names of the teachers, etc. I likewise spent several days in calling on a number of the parents and relatives, in different parts of the city, and the replies given by these parties to my inquiries fully corroborated the statements of the convicts themselves. Fifty-nine of the sixty-two criminals admitted that drinking and public-house company had not only been the chief cause of their leaving the Sunday school, but of violating the laws of their country. The number of prisoners who were tried at the Glasgow assizes in March, 1849, was 27; I visited 25 of them: 20 of the 23 who could read were old Sunday scholars, and 19 acknowledged that they had been injured by strong drink.

"The Governor of the Boys' House of Refuge, Glasgow, informs me, in a note of the 22d March, 1849, that of the 115 juvenile delinquents, 73 had been connected with Sabbath schools. He also states, that 57 of the children's fathers, and 47 mothers—total, 104—were intemperate; and 41 of the youths had been in the habit of drinking themselves. The matron of the Females' House of Refuge states, November, 28, 1848, that of the 126 inmates, including 50 unfortunate women, 105 had been connected with Sabbath schools! The matron adds, that 'intemperance is a most fruitful source of juvenile delinquency, and also of crime and profligacy in those of riper years.'

"It is scarcely necessary to remark, that these appalling facts are not adduced for the purpose of undervaluing the benevolent efforts of Sunday school teachers. On the contrary, I feel deeply interested in their disinterested labors, and have been personally identified with them for more than twenty years. My great object is to convince the friends of Sunday schools, that the accursed drinking usages of the present day are annually robbing us of thousands of young people who were once our most hopeful scholars."

[Pages might be filled with evidence to the same effect, but let the following statements by others suffice]:—The master of a large day school in the vicinity of London, stated, a few years ago, that on examining a roll containing the names of *one hundred* pupils, he ascertained upon inquiry that *ninety-one* of them had become drunkards. At *Launceston*, a similar investigation took place in a well-conducted Sabbath school, and out of *one hundred* boys, as their names stood on the register, 26 had left the neighborhood and were unknown, but of the remaining *seventy-four*, *forty* had been overcome by drunkenness!—Another says: "Of *sixty* scholars in a Sabbath school, *thirty* were found to have been ruined through drink."—Another, the Rev. W. Wight, B. A., says: "Out of a list of *eight* Sabbath school TEACHERS, *seven* were found to have been ruined through drink!" Another, a minister at Ipswich, says: "Out of *fifteen* young men professing piety and TEACHERS in the Sabbath school, *nine* were ruined through drink!"—Another, a warm friend of Sabbath schools, stated that, "In a town in Lancashire, no fewer than four 'unfortunate females' were seen together in the street, every one of whom had been once a TEACHER in a Sabbath school!"

" A few months ago a member of committee visited

one of the *singing-saloons* in Rochdale, and on a Saturday evening, about eleven o'clock, he observed about sixteen boys and girls, seated at a table in front of the stage; several of the lads had long pipes, each with a glass or jug containing intoxicating liquor, and no less than fourteen of the number were members of *Bible classes* in our different Sunday schools. There they sat, listening to the most obscene songs, witnessing scenes of the most immoral kind, and spending the interval in swallowing liquid fire." It is added: "These sinks of iniquity are thronged with old *Sunday scholars*, especially on *Sabbath evenings*, and not unfrequently until twelve o'clock." Still further it is said: "The appalling results of the drinking system are not wholly confined to the children in our schools; many a promising *teacher* has fallen a victim."

The Rev. JAMES SHERMAN, minister of the Surrey Chapel, said:—"The question has been asked, what becomes of the senior scholars of these schools? In the schools belonging to my own church the number of scholars is 3000, with 400 gratuitous teachers; but I am bound to say that few of those children become members of the church after leaving the schools. Where do they go? Many of them would be found, as soon as they arrived at the age of fifteen or sixteen, to become apprentices; and, by the pernicious system which prevailed among the working classes so situate, they grew up, many of them to be *drunkards*, and to be a disgrace to themselves and the neighborhood. A teacher of a class which was called the *vestry-class*, had collected the statistics in respert to that class, consisting of *forty-six*. He was induced to examine what were their habits in regard to Temperance during the preceding seven years, and the result was — drunkards, *thirteen;* occasional drunkards, *nine;* steady characters, thirteen; unknown, three," &c.

These are dreadful facts. They make a strong appeal to the conscience of every Christian man. They loudly call on us to do something, to do everything within our power by precept and by example, by labors and by sacrifices to put an end to an evil that in regard to thousands is turning the blessed gospel, churches, and Sabbath schools, to nought.

Almost all the crime.—P. 106.

The connection between crime and drunkenness is strikingly illustrated by the following table, which is extracted from Superintendent Linton's "Returns." It appears from this table, that nearly one half of the crimes committed, 40 per cent. of them, were committed by parties when under the influence of intoxication. Add to this percentage the number of crimes committed by those whom drink has brought to poverty—to want; whom drink has driven to desperation; whom drink has deprived of all self-respect, and all those other moral influences that keep men and women from crime; and include in the reckoning the number of crimes committed by those who have been reared in ignorance, sin, and misery, solely and entirely in consequence of the depraved and dissipated habits of their parents, and no man can doubt that drink, through its direct or indirect effects, is the pregnant cause of an overwhelming proportion of the crimes of our country.

NUMBER AND PERCENTAGE OF PERSONS APPREHENDED FOR CRIMES OR OFFENCES, WHO WERE DRUNK WHEN THEY COMMITTED THEM.

	MALES.			FEMALES.			BOTH SEXES.		
	Apprehended	Drunk when Apprehended.	Percentage Drunk.	Apprehended	Drunk when Apprehended.	Percentage Drunk.	Apprehended	Drunk when Apprehended.	Percentage Drunk.
1852	4,864	1,774	36	4,496	1,626	36	9,360	3,400	37
1853	4,620	2,914	43	4,913	1,989	40	9,533	4,003	41
1854	3,892	1,802	46	4,076	1,764	43	7,968	3,566	44
1855	3,448	1,590	46	3,711	1,491	40	7,159	3,081	43
1856	3,240	1,874	42	3,719	1,392	37	6,959	2,766	39

How is my assertion corroborated by the following statements? They are a voice from the prison. It gives forth no uncertain sound.

The *Governor of York Castle* (Jno. Noble, Esq.): "*Nineteen* out of every *twenty*, who come under my care, come, directly or indirectly, through *drinking*."

The Rev. *John Reid*, Chaplain to the Prisons of *Glasgow:* "You are desirous to know the *cause of crime* in these quarters. One short word embraces the burden of the whole matter—*Drink!* DRINK! Of at least *twenty thousand* prisoners, including juveniles, with whom I have conversed in private during the last four years, I am certain that the professedly teetotal portion of them have been *under the five hundredth* part of the whole."

James Backhouse, Esq. (the celebrated traveller in Africa): "The time of my sojourn in the Australian colonies was from the beginning of 1832 to 1838, and much of this time was occupied in visiting the prisoner population, consisting of convicts from Great Britain and Ireland. In conversing with *many thousands* of these,

I was surprised to find the *large proportion* that had fallen into crimes resulting from intemperance, and who referred to the *fines and footings* of British work-shops as their *first step* in this evil course."

Twelfth Report of the Inspectors of Prisons: " On the question being put to a number of prisoners in *Edinburgh* gaol, under twenty years of age—' What do you assign as the first cause of your falling into error?' '*Drink*' is almost the invariable answer."

Rev. *George Hislop*, Chaplain to prison of *Edinburgh:* "I am unable to mark out, with arithmetical precision, the place among the causes of crime which must be assigned to this habit (*intemperance*); but I have no hesitation in expressing the opinion that it is one of the *most active*, and, at present, the *most prevalent* of secondary causes."

Rev. *H. Meeres*, Chaplain of *Rochester* gaol: "I have no hesitation in saying that a *very* large proportion, possibly nineteen out of every twenty, are imprisoned through the effects of *drunkenness*."

Rev. *W. Brown*, General Prison, *Perth:* "Our prisoners in general are, directly or indirectly, the victims of *intemperance*."

Rev. *Geo. M'Lear*, Chaplain, *Bedford* gaol: "My experience of eighteen years justifies the conclusion that ninety-nine out of every hundred owe their imprisonment, directly or indirectly, to *intemperance*."—"New prisons and new regulations will, humanly speaking, be of little benefit, so long as *intemperance* prevails to the extent it now does."

APPENDIX.

The legislature may render essential service.—P. 107.

The combined influence of legislative enactments, of the reduction of public houses, of total abstinence principles, and of that elevation of public feeling and morals, which is mainly to be attributed to the attention which temperance societies have turned to the subject of drunkenness, and to the light which they have thrown upon the extent and evils of this vice, appears in the improved habits of the people, as very strikingly brought out in the following tables. They demonstrate that sobriety is on the increase, and drunkenness on the wane. These tables are extracted from "Returns as to Crimes, Offences, and Contraventions, and to cases of Drunkenness," prepared for the Magistrates and Council by Mr. Linton, Superintendent of Police.

NUMBER OF PERSONS FOUND DRUNK IN THE STREETS, AND KEPT IN THE POLICE OFFICE AND STATION-HOUSES TILL THEY WERE SOBER, AND NUMBER WHO WERE DRUNK WHEN APPREHENDED FOR CRIMES AND OFFENCES.

Total Number taken Charge of by the Police.

	MALES.			FEMALES.			BOTH SEXES.		
	Found Drunk and kept till Sober.	Drunk when Apprehended.	Total.	Found Drunk and kept till Sober.	Drunk when Apprehended.	Total.	Found Drunk and kept till Sober.	Drunk when Apprehended.	Total.
1852	3,903	1,774	5,677	2,464	1,626	4,090	6,367	3,400	9,767
1853	3,460	2,014	5,474	2,267	1,989	4,256	5,727	4,003	9,730
1854	3,126	1,802	4,928	2,057	1,764	3,821	5,183	3,566	8,749
1855	2,993	1,590	4,583	2,021	1,491	3,512	5,014	3,081	8,095
1856	2,847	1,374	4,221	2,123	1,392	3,515	4,970	2,766	7,736

It were much to be desired that this country, which in the last and in the beginning of the present century devoted more than twenty years, all its energies, and many hundred millions of money to wars that have not prevented a Bonaparte from occupying the throne of France, and which I may say devoted other twenty years to fighting the battles of political reform, would now (Providence permitting) devote at least twenty years, and all the millions that might be needed for such a purpose, to the grand object of social reforms—such as sanitary improvements, the universal education of the people, promotion of temperance, and, through many other means, the comforts and elevation of the working classes, and the elevation especially of the sunken classes of society.

In reference to the great social evil of intemperance, a beginning has been made—something has been done—but much yet remains to be done, much—and that the better part also—which the legislators cannot do. Our main hope lies in raising the tone of public feeling and opinion, and that by means of the intellectual, moral, and religious elevation of the people. We would, however, venture to suggest, for the consideration of our legislators, the following measures. They would do much to remove temptation out of the way of the people, and check the growth and progress of intemperance :—

1. Until public-houses, opened for the mere purpose of drinking, are declared illegal, because carrying on a traffic pernicious to the interests of the community, a law should be passed, requiring these to be closed at an early hour in the evening, as they are now by law kept shut to a late hour in the morning. The keeping of them shut till eight in the morning has preserved many a poor

man from temptation when on the road to his work—the closing of them at six o'clock at night would do still more good, by preserving many a working man from temptation when his day's work was over. They should be made to resemble the ash-tree, which is the last to open up its leaves, and one of the first to close them.

2. All places opened for the mere purpose of drinking intoxicating liquors should be declared illegal, as in most cases the ruin of the poor and a curse to the community. If some will drink, they have wife and children, brothers and sisters, at home, to prevent their drinking to excess, or becoming slaves to the habit. The interest of the dram-seller, on the other hand, lies in inducing them to become frequent and regular customers of his shop. The more they drink, and the deeper they drink, the worse for their families, but the better for him.

3. The law should regard every man or woman, who can be proved before a jury or any other proper authority, to be in habit and repute a drunkard, as a lunatic, and deal with them accordingly. The prospect of a shaven head, a strait jacket (if needful), the high walls of an asylum, and the society of the insane, would strike men with salutary terror. Months of sobriety would, in many instances, so restore the brain and body to health, that the person would acquire the power of resisting temptation, and come out to drink no more—the slave would acquire freedom in the house of bondage. That should be done according to law which is done without law; for it is well known that, within the House of Refuge here, and in other places elsewhere, hundreds of poor drunkards are shut up. Some go to be cured by entire removal from temptation, some consent to go dur-

ing a fit of temporary penitence, when under the remorse of *delirium tremens;* but, however they go, fortunately for their families, society, and themselves, they find it easier to get in than get out. I have known many parents disgraced and tormented by a drunken son, many wives maltreated by drunken husbands, whose cruelty they had not only to bear, but whom their industry had to support, and not a few husbands whose life was embittered, and whose property was wasted, and whose children were neglected and ruined, through the dissipated habits of the mother of the house. To all these, what a relief would such a law as I suggest bring? I know a man in a respectable position in this town, who, to prevent his wife selling his silver spoons and pawning his clothes and furniture, made her a regular allowance of two bottles of whisky per day—and she drank them. In all such cases the law ought to give relief in justice to a good as against an evil doer. It is strange to see how society stands by and allows so many to waste their life, their wages, their substance on drink, and thereby throw the burden of maintaining their families on the sober and industrious part of the community. Virtue with us is taxed to support vice.

4. As the drunkard is held responsible for all that he does in a state of drunkenness, the law should declare that the keeper of the drinking-shop within which he got drunk shall share in his responsibility. No man can have a right, for the sake of money, to convert another man into a madman, and, having turned him out on society, to say, of whatever offence in his madness he commits, "my hands are clean."

5. The drunkard who deprives himself of reason, and

thereby makes himself capable of committing any crime, should, in all cases, be regarded as a subject of punishment; and the keeper of the drinking-shop, who supplied him, should be punished as equally guilty with himself—in many instances as more so.

6. Our legislators should contrive some means at law whereby those who create the poverty of the country should be made upon their own shoulders to carry the burden of it. For illustration's sake, take this case:— I knew a man who left a public-house drunk on a Saturday night, and on Sabbath morning was found smashed, stiff and dead, at the foot of a crag, by the side of which his path homewards lay. The burden of supporting that man's family ought to have been laid, not upon the public, but upon the publican; and the principles of such a law should be carried out to its fullest possible extent.

Some plead for better lodgings and sanitary measures.—P. 108.

The urgent necessity of these in Edinburgh is powerfully brought out in a letter addressed to the Lord Provost and Magistrates, by Henry Johnston, Esq., H.E.I.C.S., and in a pamphlet which that gentleman has published on the state of our closes and by-streets. He exposes to those who never turn a foot in the way of these abodes of foul wretchedness and misery a state of matters ruinous to the public health, pernicious to public morals, and a disgrace to our capital and its inhabitants.

Dr. George Bell published some years ago an account of the houses and inhabitants of Blackfriars' Wynd, which presents a most doleful view of the sin, misery, wretchedness, and foulness of some parts of our city.

But the necessity of sanitary measures could not be better brought out than by the following extracts from a report given last summer by Dr. Letheby, to the City Commissioners of Sewers for London:

"I have also been at much pains during the last three months to ascertain the precise conditions of the dwellings, the habits, and the diseases of the poor. In this way, 2208 rooms have been most circumstantially inspected, and the general result is, that nearly all of them are filthy, or over-crowded, or imperfectly drained, or badly ventilated, or out of repair. In 1989 of these rooms, all, in fact, that are at present inhabited, there are 5791 inmates, belonging to 1576 families; and to say nothing of the too frequent occurrence of what may be regarded as a necessitous over-crowding, where the husband, the wife, and young family of four or five children are cramped into a miserably small and ill-conditioned room, there are numerous instances where adults of both sexes, belonging to different families, are lodged in the same room, regardless of all the common decencies of life, and where from three to five adults, men and women, besides a train or two of children, are accustomed to herd together like brute beasts or savages; and where every human instinct of propriety or decency are smothered. Like my predecessor, I have seen grown persons of both sexes sleeping in common with their parents, brothers, and sisters, and cousins, and even the casual acquaintance of a day's tramp occupying the same bed of filthy rags or straw; a woman suffering in travail, in the midst of males and females of

APPENDIX. 193

different families that tenant the same room; where birth and death go hand in hand; where the child but newly born, the patient cast down with fever, and the corpse waiting for interment, have no separation from each other, or from the rest of the inmates. Of the many cases to which I have alluded, there are some that have commanded my attention by reason of their unusual depravity—cases in which from three to four adults of both sexes, with many children, were lodging in the same room, and often sleeping in the same bed. I have note of three or four localities where 48 men, 73 women, and 59 children are living in 34 rooms. In one room there are 2 men, 3 women, and 5 children; and in another 1 man, 4 women, and 2 children; and when, about a fortnight since, I visited the back room on the ground floor of No. 5, I found it occupied by 1 man, 2 women, and 2 children; and in it was the dead body of a poor girl, who had died in childbirth a few days before. The body was stretched out on the bare floor, without shroud or coffin. There it lay in the midst of the living, and we may well ask how it can be otherwise than that the human heart should be deadened to all the gentler feelings of our nature, when such sights as these are of common occurrence.

"So close and unwholesome is the atmosphere of some of the rooms, that I have endeavored to ascertain, by chemical means, whether it does not contain some peculiar product of decomposition, that gives to it its foul odor and its rare powers of engendering disease. I find that it is not only deficient in the due proportion of oxygen, but it contains three times the usual amount of carbonic acid, besides a quantity of aqueous vapor charged with alkaline matter that stinks abominably. This is, doubtless, the product of putrefaction and of the various fœtid and stagnant exhalations that pollute the air of the place. In many of my former reports, and in those of my predecessor, your attention has been drawn to this pestilential source of disease, and to the consequence of heaping human beings into such contracted localities; and I again revert to it because of its great importance, not merely that it perpetuates fever and the allied disorders, but because there stalks side by side with this pestilence a yet deadlier presence, blighting the moral existence of a rising population, rendering their hearts hopeless, their acts ruffianly and incestuous, and scattering, while society averts her eye, the retributive seeds of increase for crime, turbulence, and pauperism."

All who are familiar with the homes of the poorer and the haunts of the wicked and lapsed classes, will be reminded by this report of scenes which they themselves have witnessed in our large cities.

Before the Statistical Society at Liverpool, in September, 1837, Mr. Langton read a paper on the inhabited courts and cellars in Liverpool. The courts were 2271, and the cellars 7493; dark, damp, confined, and tenanted by nearly 30,000 souls.

In 1838, Mr. James Heywood read a paper before the Statistical Society of London, giving an account of a house-to-house visitation, of 176 families in Manchester. 165 houses contained many cellars, and there were 11 separate cellars.

In 1847 a committee of the Statistical Society of London inspected the dwellings, room by room, and condition of the inhabitants, of Church Lane, St. Giles, London. The population examined was 463, the number of families 100, and the number of bedsteads among them 90. There was an average, therefore, of above 5 persons to 1 bed; and many rooms were inhabited by as many as 22 souls. They report that " in these wretched dwellings all ages and both sexes, fathers and daughters, mothers and sons, grown-up brothers and sisters, stranger adult males and females, and swarms of children, the sick, the dying, and the dead, are herded together with a proximity and mutual pressure which brutes would resist; where it is physically impossible to preserve the ordinary decencies of life; where all sense of propriety and self-respect must be lost, to be replaced only by a recklessness of demeanor which necessarily results from vitiated minds; and yet with many of the young, brought up in such hot-beds of mental pestilence, the hopeless, but benevolent attempt is making to implant, by means of general education, the seeds of religion, virtue, truth, order, industry, and cleanliness; but which seeds, to fructify advantageously, need, it is to be feared, a soil far less rank than can be found in these wretched abodes. Tender minds, once vitiated, present almost insuperable difficulties to reformation; bad habits and depraved feelings gather with the growth, and strengthen with the strength."

In what large town in the kingdom are not many of the poorer classes of the people living in circumstances which outrage all decency, destroy every moral feeling, and, of necessity, lead to debasement, dissipation, and crime?

196   APPENDIX.

The principle of temperance, as I hold it.—P. 118.

For a luminous and powerful exposition of the principle of temperance, as held by the writer of these sermons, he would refer the reader to a lecture delivered in London, by Professor James Miller of this city, and entitled "Abstinence, its Place, and Power."

We do nothing to instruct them, &c. We first condemn them to crime, and then condemn them to punishment.—P. 137.

The following statistics, like all others of the same description, plainly show how intimately crime is connected with ignorance, and what a total want of education exists amongst the lowest class, which furnish by far the larger number of the criminals of our country.

EXTRACT from the CRIMINAL STATISTICS and RETURNS of the MANCHESTER POLICE.

The following is a table of the age of the persons taken into custody, with the degree of instruction, for the nine months ending 30th September, 1856:—

No.	Under 10 years of age.	10 years and under 15.	15 years and under 20.	Above 20 years of age.
4470	10	418	963	3079

DEGREE OF INSTRUCTION OF THESE 4470.

Neither able to read or write.	Read only, or read and write imperfectly.	Read and write well.	Superior instruction.
1748	2623	108	1

PER CENTAGE.

Total.	Of the uneducated.	Of the imperfectly educated.	Of the well and superior educated.
4470	38·99	58·68	2·32

In regard to by far the largest proportion of those entered in the column of the imperfectly educated, so far as all practical purposes and the benefits of education are concerned, they might with propriety be entered under the head of not educated at all; for it has always been found that those who could not read but with difficulty did not read at all, and were as completely shut out from such means of improvement as books afforded as those who do not know the letters.

There are thousands, and tens of thousands, and hundreds of thousands, of the children of this land, who are growing up strangers to the benefits and blessings of education. Ignorance is their sole, sad inheritance. They are punished for it, impoverished for it, imprisoned for it, banished for it, and hanged for it.—P. 139.

For full proof of this statement, we refer to the Government census on education.

The low state of education in Birmingham, where infant labor is remunerative, and where thousands of poor children are found at work who ought to be at school, is strikingly brought out by the fact that fourteen months is the full average time which the working classes of Birmingham spend at school.

In regard to Glasgow, we have been told that Mr. Strang, the great statist of Glasgow, calculates that there are from 6000 to 7000 children in that city, between 5 and 10 years of age, who are not attending any school. Captain Smart, the very intelligent superintendent of police in that city, reckons that the number of these children will exceed 10,000. A remarkably able, and intelligent gentleman, who has given much attention to philanthropic subjects, writes me in reference to Glasgow:—"I have had occasion to observe, since the Registration Act came into operation, that while bastardy is common among mill-workers, the inability to write is equally common. The number of uneducated adults is very great. It is of great importance to observe that the schools are unequally distributed. I find that in twelve districts, containing 12,194 habitually non-church-going families, there are no schools; and these districts include streets teeming with 'ragged boys.'" Now, these figures, which I believe are correct, square with others upon which I place more reliance. The Tron parish, which may be regarded as a medium example of the parishes which contain the bulk of the poor population, contains 2200 families, and estimating each family at nearly 6 individuals, which I believe is a truer estimate than $4\frac{1}{3}$, the population of this parish is 13,500. In this parish there are 3 schools, and at these schools there are not more than 500 children. But each family can supply a child between 5 and 11 years of age, and thus there is only a fraction of the children at school. This district contains many of the city Arab tribe. How credible, Dr. Bell adds, is the remark which Mr. M'Callum, the admirable Superintendent of the Reformatory School, made to me:—" It is a rare thing to meet with an educated juvenile criminal; as a class they are deplorably ignorant."

That the want of education is far greater in Glasgow than any thing which Mr. Strang or the superintendent of police has conjectured—for these gentlemen do not profess to do any thing more than hazard a conjecture—will appear by looking into the state of another large manufacturing town, where the Education question has been keenly discussed for many years, and the truth connected with it thoroughly expiscated. I refer to Manchester; and as is Manchester, I have no doubt, so are almost all our large manufacturing towns. Our demand for Educational legislation, extension, and improvement, is sometimes met by the statement that we have made such progress with our present means and machinery, that it is best to let things alone, and that in the course of years the evil will be completely met. In many parts of the country, no doubt, much progress in a right direction has been made, but apart altogether from the case of the thousands and hundreds of thousands whom the let-alone system consigns to ruin, until it grows adequate to the wants of the country, on the very improbable supposition that it would ever do so, it is not the fact that the state of matters is getting better in our large towns under the present system. The fact is, that notwithstanding all the exertions made under the present plan to meet the evil and make headway, with all the steam up, we are going astern in our large manufacturing towns; the evil is growing worse and worse. That appears from the following table, extracted from the Manchester and Salford Statistical Society's Reports:—

Year.	In Manchester, Salford, Broughton, and Pendleton.		Proportion. One in
	Day School Attendance. Total, public and private.	Population.	
1834–5	24,365	250,373	10,27
1851	29,145	307,816	13,80

It appears, therefore, in respect to day-school attendance, at the present time, it is worse than it was 17 years ago; inasmuch as from 1834–5 to 1851, day-school attendance, considered in relation to the population, has decreased from 1 in every 10 to 1 in 13 odds.

The following Table gives us the educational wants of Manchester, as ascertained in 1851; and taking that town as a standard by which to judge of our great centres of manufacture, it is dreadful to think of the total number of children in this kingdom whom our present system leaves parents, in so many instances, to bring up to the curses, and miseries, and crimes of ignorance—a disgrace, a danger, and a burden to the community.

ESTIMATED NUMBER OF CHILDREN OF THE WORKING CLASSES, BETWEEN 3 AND 15, NEITHER "AT SCHOOL," NOR "AT WORK."

CENSUS RETURNS. (Evidence, p. 470.)		PRIVATE INQUIRY, INCLUDING CHILDREN NOT IN THE CENSUS RETURNS. (Evidence, pp. 359, 361.)	
Total No. of Children under 15	130,608	Total No. of Children between 3 and 15..........	99,193
" under 3........	32,118		
Total Number of Children between 3 and 15........	98,490	Children of all classes attending school...	34,073
Total No. receiving *any kind of daily instruction*.. 44,598		Children not at school, but *supposed to belong to the middle and upper classes*, at home, in employment, or receiving private education.. 10,450	
Under 3....... 634			
Total receiving *any kind of daily instruction*, between 3 and 15............ 43,964		(*Assume* four fifths *of children* "in employment" (*Census Table*) *to belong to the working classes*)................ 11,728	
Children of all classes in employment (*same age*)........ 14,660			
" Children receiving instruction," or "at work"......	58,624	Children "*at school*" or "*at work*"...............	56,251
Children not described as "receiving instruction" either "at home" or "at school," or "in employment"..................	39,866	Children *of the working classes* not "at school" nor "at work"...............	42,942

REMARKS ON THE CENSUS RETURNS.

1. These returns include all children whom the different parties that made the returns *considered to be receiving any kind of daily instruction,* either "under a master or governess at home," or by attending school.

2. The better educated classes of society would generally make such returns pretty correctly; and, therefore, comparatively few of the children of these classes

will be found among such, as in the above table, are "undescribed."

3. The less educated and many of the working classes are known to have very lax notions respecting school attendance; and, therefore, the returns from those classes may be considered to be much exaggerated.

4. And consequently it is probable that the number of children "undescribed" will fall short of *the whole number of children of the working classes* ALONE, *who, though not prevented by "work," are not "attending day school."*

REMARKS ON THE PRIVATE INQUIRY.

1. The number of "children attending school" exceeds by 5358 the corresponding returns of the census, *Ev.* p. 475; although the total number of children in this Table exceeds that with which it is compared by only 703 children; and therefore this Table makes a very liberal representation of the total school attendance.

2. No evidence has been adduced to show that the additional number (22,178) here taken to represent the children of the *middle and upper classes* " at home" or " in employment," together with those of the *working classes* "in employment," is likely to be below the actual number.

3. And, consequently, the statements in ths Tablei representing the average number of children of the working classes neither "at school" nor "in employment," have no less claim for consideration than the Census Table, although it appears to differ in the result.

It has been stated in evidence (pages 360, 391) that about "54,670 *children belonging to the laboring classes, whether employed or not, are not attending day schools,*" and that no reason has been alleged, that ought to be considered satisfactory, why "one half, at least," of that number ought not "to be in some school receiving education." It is indeed highly probable that, at the present time, there are not fewer than 20,000 or 30,000 children of the laboring classes kept from day school, without being in employment or detained at home through sickness, domestic need, or any other sufficient cause, and who ought therefore to be gathered into school.

The most extraordinary errors may lurk under general statistics; the public, judging by them alone, may cherish the delusion that all is right when much is wrong.—P. 143.

How easily statistical facts, unless regarded in all their bearings, may be the means of producing a false impression, is illustrated by the following Table. Looking only at the increase of attendance at the Church of England, British, and Denominational Schools, one would infer a great improvement in the educational state of Manchester; but further inquiry shows, that what one class of schools has gained another has lost; that the scholars have not increased as they should have done, but only shifted their ground.

From that Table, also, it will be seen, that while the attendance at Church and Denominational Schools has *increased* since 1834–5, from 5434 to 16,367, the attendance at Private Schools, of all classes, has *decreased* from 18,465 to 11,713. And hence it appears that the increased attendance at Public Schools is to be attributed

APPENDIX.

in a much greater degree to the withdrawing of children from Private Schools, than to the bringing of additional children under the influence of education.

This circumstance is the more important when taken in connection with the fact, that the increase of school attendance during the last 17 years has fallen short considerably of the increase of the population.

Class of Schools	1834-5. Actual Attendance. M. and S. Statistical Society's Report.			1851. Average Attendance. Census Returns.			1851. Connected with the Schools. Private Inquiry.		
	Manchester.*	Salford, Broughton, and Pendleton.†	Total.	Manchester.	Salford, Broughton, and Pendleton.	Total.	Manchester.	Salford, Broughton, and Pendleton.	Total.
Grammar Schools	200	..	200	322	..	322	380	..	380
Private Schools of every class	14,226	4,239	18,465	9,139	2,574	11,718	8,106	2,186	10,292
Church of England, British and Denominational Schools	3,828	1,606	5,434	12,990	3,377	16,367	17,129	4,193	21,322
Mill Schools, Workhouse, Prison, and other Schools	96	170	266	494	249	‡743	494	249	‡743
Total Attendance in every class of Schools	18,350	6,015	24,365	22,945	6,200	29,145	26,109	6,628	32,737

* Omitting *Newton.* † Omitting *Pendlebury.*
‡ Omitted in the Total given in the Census Returns, see Ev. p. 359.

Note.—If to the Total here given (32,737), there be added 629 children in *Pendlebury* and 707 in extra-municipal Institutions, the result will be 34,073, as Ev. p. 359.— (*Private Inquiry.*)

While it is the duty of the state to provide the means of education, it is no less her duty to see that they are used.—P. 144.

It appears to us plain that society should charge itself with the duty of promptly meeting the educational wants of our country. The very existence of Britain's power and position, the interests of religion, the welfare of the nation, are involved in this subject. The question of a complete religious education belongs to the churches; the question of such an education as shall make men useful members of society belongs to the state; and while we would strongly deprecate a secular system of education, excluding the leading principles of a common Christianity from our common schools; unless the different denominations will so agree to make that practicable, they will drive men into the secular system; for surely better that these poor children should get some instruction than that they be left without any knowledge—to live, and sin, and die uninstructed as the brutes that perish.

It is a scandal to the churches that there should be any difficulty found in agreeing on a system of religious instruction suitable to little children. We are sure that that difficulty has no foundation in the Word of God. What have these infants to do with those ecclesiastical and doctrinal questions which unhappily divide good men among us? If we that are adults can always join in private worship with each other, and on occasions in public worship, and even sit down at the Lord's table with each other, recognising amid all our differences a common brotherhood and a common faith, it were a melancholy thing indeed if we cannot agree about the simple elements of religion that are to be taught to little children; and that this wretched difficulty should be an obstruction in the way of that national system of education which the state is bound to establish, and without which no voluntary efforts will ever meet the wants of the country.

It should encourage Government and the Parliament to know that the people belonging to the different denominations do not sympathise with the extremer views of their ministers, and that they would heartily rejoice in the establishment of a system of education which would meet the wants of the country, although it did not meet the views and demands of those ecclesiastics who would perversely sacrifice the interests of the people to their own crotchets, love of power, or denominational peculiarities.

So long as this is—what, no doubt, it will ever be—a Protestant country, the Protestant religion should be that of national schools; but communicated in such a way as to give complete freedom to the consciences of Roman Catholics, or any other party declining to receive the religious instruction provided in the public schools. The children of Roman Catholic parents may be allowed to leave the school at the time of religious instruction; or whenever, if such a system should be preferred, there were a sufficient number of Roman Catholics as to furnish children for a school supported out of the public funds, let these be applied to giving secular instruction only—the religious education of the Roman Catholic Church being left to parents or priests. Thus the country would secure that all these children receive a good secular education, and the country would not be employing the public funds in the propagation of what this Protestant kingdom regards as dangerous errors.

Whatever arrangement the state may make as to these matters, one thing she is entitled and bound to do, and that is this, to require that every child within her bounds shall be educated. If the parents are able but unwilling to do that, they should be compelled to do it—punished if they don't do it. If they are not able to do that, then it should be done at the public expense. To make sure that this is done, a system of inspection should be established. Such a system would not be found to interfere in the least degree with the rights and liberties of those who do their duty to their children and to the state; like other arrangements and laws for the preserving of honesty and order, that system would only be a terror, and a check, and a yoke to "evil-doers." People might send their children to public schools or private schools, national or denominational schools; but the state is entitled to see that they are receiving at least a plain education at some school.

The state is called on to extend the law to all manufactures, work, and service, which applies at present to the flax and cotton mills. Why should the children laboring in these manufactories enjoy a protection denied to others? what is good for them is good for others; what was needed by them is needed by thousands and tens of thousands of the children whose education is neglected, and whose best interests are sacrificed to the profits of their masters and the cupidity of their parents. The state should require, as it does in other countries, that no child be allowed to engage in any kind of remunerative labor until it has received a plain education, or unless arrangements are made, while it is engaged in service or in manufacture, to conduct and complete its education by so many hours a-day being set apart to that purpose.

It is a most interesting fact that John Knox—in whose eye education bulked so large, that at the Reformation he proposed that one-fourth and more of the whole of the immense revenues of the Roman Catholic Church (the greater part of which were devoured by the Crown and nobles) should be sacredly devoted to the purpose of educating the children of the nation—three hundred years ago laid down the very principle which we advocate, and which is carried into practical effect with so much advantage in some parts of the Continent. It reflects immortal honor on the memory of that great man, that the education of the people was with him a first object; one to be striven for most resolutely, and paid for most liberally; and that he had the far-seeing eye to discern the great principle on which the working of the system should be based,—viz., the right and duty of the state to require that every child within its bounds shall receive such an education as to make it a useful member of society. He has embodied that in these words, extracted from the First Book of Discipline, which was laid before the Great Council of Scotland in 1560:—" This must be carefully provided, that no father, of what state or condition that ever he be, use his children at his own fantasie, especially in their youth-head; but all must be compelled to bring up their children in learning and virtue."

In the United States of America, by one of their last reports, complaints appear to come from every part of the country that parents neglect to send their children to school.—P. 144.

See the Twentieth Annual Report of the Board of Education, published at Boston, 1857.

What an appaling picture of irreligion do our large towns present!—P. 151.

EDINBURGH.—The Report of the Royal Commissioners on Religious Instruction proclaimed the fact, that one-third of the entire population of Edinburgh, or 50,000 people, had no fixed connection with any Christian Church.

GLASGOW.—In this city the proportion of its inhabitants which should be found attending church is, at the lowest computation, above 200,000. The whole amount of church accommodation there is for 140,000. So that if all the churches were filled to overflowing, there would still be more than 60,000 in that city who were attending no house of God. But one of the most benevolent and intelligent and Christian merchants of Glasgow informed me that many of the churches are not more than half filled; so that we may consider ourselves as making a very moderate calculation in concluding that more than 100,000 people in the city of Glasgow are living in a state of practical heathenism in this Christian land.

These calculations are corroborated by the statistics of the City Mission, published in February, 1856. It appears from this document that they have divided the city into 54 districts, and that in these districts there are 25,546 families who are on the whole non-church-going, and 15,675 families who never enter a church. These are nominally Protestants. It is estimated by them that each family consists of $4\frac{1}{3}$ individuals; and thus there are 110,699 individuals who are on the whole non-church-going, and 67,925 who never enter a church.

An admirable Report, entitled "Mission Churches of the United Presbyterian Church in Glasgow," fully bears out the preceding statements. From a thorough examination of the state of the city, and careful calculations, they arrive at this conclusion, that in Glasgow there are "in addition to the Roman Catholics, 100,204 persons living in open contempt of the ordinances of religion. The astounding fact is thus reached, that we are living in the midst of 180,000 fellow-citizens, popish and heathen, that is, *one-half of our entire population* who stand in pressing need of our missionary exertions."

LONDON AND ITS DISTRICTS some years ago contained a population of 2,434,868. The city was increasing annually at the rate of 25,000. The accommodation provided in the churches of all denominations would not accommodate one-third of the whole population; and although these were all full to overflowing, London would contain 649,297 living in a state of practical heathenism. But it is a notorious fact that a great many of the churches in the metropolis are miserably thin; and there can be no doubt of the truth of the terrible statement, that more than One Million of the people of London are living in the habit of neglecting the worship and house of God.

We have had already fruit of our labors.—P. 154.

The following statement regarding the Pleasance Territorial Mission was published by my colleague, the Rev. Dr. Hanna, to whose zeal and labors under God, this interesting and important work owes much of its existence and success.

Pleasance Territorial Mission.

"This mission has now been in operation for about four years. During that time we have succeeded in getting almost evey child of proper age within the district marked out for our operations, to attend our schools. There were nearly 200 children in that position when we began our work. There are not now more than half a dozen. Our success in this department has been complete. To realize it, we had to buy a site and build a school-house, at a cost of upwards of £600, and we had to give good salaries to our schoolmaster and schoolmistress. But it was not the building of the schoolhouse, nor the providing of a good education for all who chose to seek it, which accomplished the great object we had in view, namely, the bringing those children to school who otherwise would have grown up uneducated. It was the repeated visits of the missionary, and of the lady agents to the homes of the people, explaining to them the benefits which the school erected in their neighborhood was fitted to confer upon their families, and urging those who had children of the right age to send them there to be taught, which realized that end; and it is by such means alone that the uneducated children of the lowest class of our population can ever be gathered into the school-house.

"But it is far easier, within any district, to bring every child to school than every adult to church, especially where neglect of divine ordinances has been of long continuance, and is the prevailing habit of the stair, or close, or street, in which such forsakers of the sanctuary are congregated. To reclaim such to habits of church-going is the most difficult thing to which Christian benevolence can put its hands. Concentrated and sustained effort, much patience and many prayers, are all required. But our labors in this department also have not been without good fruit. A small congregation, composed almost entirely of those who had been living in entire neglect of divine ordinances, has been gathering. For the last three years the ordinance of the Lord's Supper has been regularly dispensed. One hundred and twelve individuals have been admitted to the fellowship of the Church. Fifty of these had never been in connection with any Church; so many as thirty-three of whom were far advanced in life. There were forty-seven, with some of whom it had been ten, with some twenty, with some thirty years since they had sat down at the table of the Lord; leaving only fifteen out of the hundred and twelve who were in full communion when they joined our little congregation. The ordinary attendance at puplic worship, which began with about a dozen, now averages from eighty to a hundred in the forenoon, and from a hundred to a hundred and sixty in the afternoon.

"The school-room in which the services have been held is now quite full. We have arrived at that stage when, unless a church and a minister be provided, but little further progress can be made. We are as far on— we have as many communicants and as large an attendance, as any of those territorial missions in whose steps we are following had, when churches and ministers were provided for them. It is our intention to apply to the Church Courts to have Mr. Cochrane, our present missionary, licensed and ordained as the minister of that little flock which he has gathered in from the wilderness. At a meeting lately, held with them, the communicants expressed this to be their unanimous and most earnest desire. It remains only that we provide a suitable place of worship. It has been resolved that upon this building there shall be no debt, and that beyond the present there shall be no second application made. Whatever be the sum put into the hands of the Committee appointed by the Session, they are resolved not to go a farthing beyond it in their expenditure. We have, however, not only a church to build, we must either enlarge our infant school-room or erect a more commodious one. The Government Inspector of Schools has imposed upon us the condition either of doing this, or of dismissing a number of the children, which we cannot make up our minds to do. Without venturing to assign any scale of giving, it is our earnest hope that, by one effort of generosity, we may be enabled to perfect the external apparatus of this mission, and so put it in condition for making that further and still greater progress which we can have no doubt that, when so furnished, it will, with the divine blessing, speedily realize."

We are now about to build a regular place of worship in this locality, and to form the people into a regular congregation under an ordained minister; and as we must raise £1000 at least to meet the expenses of the building, the public are earnestly solicited to lend us a helping hand. Any money sent to the Rev. Dr. Hanna, Castle Terrace, or the Rev. Dr. Guthrie, Salisbury Road, Edinburgh, will be gratefully received. We need sympathy and support, and we hope for them.

The work would be found to be perfectly practicable.
—Pp. 156, 157.

On this subject the Rev. Mr. Bonar, one of the ministers of the Canongate, in a pamphlet full of startling facts and earnest pleading, which he has just published, makes the following statement in reference to the case of the West-Port Territorial Church, which is all the more valuable not only as given by a clergyman who is thoroughly acquainted with the condition of the lower classes, but who belongs to a different church from those who have so successfully cultivated that district of our city:—" So far from being utopian, the plan indicated has been justified by actual results. In one of the very worst localities of Edinburgh, to which, only a few years before, an infamous notoriety attached, in which, upon survey, it was found that in the main streets and adjoining wynds, out of 411 families, only 45 were attached to any Christian communion, 70 were Roman Catholics, and 296 were entirely unconnected with any church; wherein, out of a gross population of 2000, 1500 were living strangers to the observance of religion, and in which 290 children were growing up wholly untaught; a district in which the moral and physical condition of the community was most deplorable, one fourth being paupers and another fourth street-beggars, thieves, and prostitutes;—in this locality a wonderful change has been brought about. The West-Port was divided into twenty districts, each containing twenty families. A school was opened—not on the system of gratuitous instruction—first of all, at the end of the close where the atrocities of Burke and Hare had been committed, in an old deserted tannery, approached by a flight of wooden steps. At the outset appearances were abundantly unpromising, and on the first occasion, after the advices, requests, and entreaties which had for many previous weeks been brought to bear upon those whose highest good was contemplated and desired, only about a dozen adults, and these chiefly old women, were present. Now there is a substantial church, well attended, and not long since enlarged by the addition of a gallery; schools, week-day and evening, largely attended likewise, with the other desiderata of a library and a savings-bank, a washing-house, and a female industrial school. The problem has been solved. An instance was afforded, to adopt the words of Dr. Chalmers' biographer, ' in which the depths of city ignorance and vice have been sounded to the very bottom; nor can the possibility of cleansing the foul basement storey of our social edifice be doubted any longer.' Nor do we wonder that the great Christian philanthropist—for so he must be regarded by all unprejudiced minds—hailed what he was spared to see as ' the streaks and dawnings of a better day,' and was willing, ' after the struggles and discomfitures of thirty years,' to ' depart in peace, and leave the further prosecution with comfort and calmness in the hands of another generation.' "

www.ingramcontent.com/pod-product-compliance
Lightning Source LLC
LaVergne TN
LVHW021617040625
813025LV00009B/361